Stirring praise for Davis Phinney and

THE HAPPINESS OF PURSUIT

"In this touching personal account, Davis provides inspiration to the millions of families worldwide — mine included — who join the Phinneys in never giving up hope that we'll find a cure for this disease."

—U.S. Senator Mark Udall

"Davis Phinney always brought great intensity to his racing, which propelled him to the pinnacle of the sport and which now drives him as he confronts his disease. *The Happiness of Pursuit* is a fabulous story of courage — a must-read."

—Jim Ochowicz, general manager, BMC Racing Team

"*The Happiness of Pursuit* tells the incredible story of Davis Phinney, one of the most talented riders of his generation, with a career marked by many successes. When he was diagnosed with Parkinson's disease he faced the challenge with the same determination, courage, and willpower he demonstrated as a world-class bicycle racer. For Phinney, every step in his son Taylor's cycling journey has been a great joy, a victory, and perhaps a fulfillment of destiny."

—Eddy Merckx, former professional cyclist
and five-time Tour de France winner

"What happens when you take an amazing family of athletes and bring in one of America's best writers to capture their stories of achievement, perseverance, and hope? You get an instant classic."
— **Bob Babbitt, cofounder and editor in chief, *Competitor***

"Davis Phinney and Taylor Phinney. Father and son. They have in common an incredible drive to succeed. *The Happiness of Pursuit* shows how a father and son can become an unbeatable combination, building a strong relationship by conquering challenges both on and off the bike."
— **Axel Merckx, former professional cyclist and current team director of Trek-Livestrong U23**

"The cycling talent scouts' salivary glands went into hyperdrive when they saw Davis Phinney for the first time. But what they slowly came to understand was that the era of the pedestaled despot was over. The untouchable tyrants like Hinault, Saronni, Moser, and Roche would have to yield to more democratic leaders. Davis Phinney heralded a more open, clean, and passionate sport that we now see having worldwide appeal. It was my great fortune to have been a teammate of Davis, who is one of the cornerstones of my personal passion and enjoyment of our sport."
— **Bob Roll, cycling commentator**

THE HAPPINESS OF PURSUIT

THE HAPPINESS
OF PURSUIT

*A Father's Courage, a Son's Love,
and Life's Steepest Climb*

DAVIS PHINNEY

with Austin Murphy

HOUGHTON MIFFLIN HARCOURT BOSTON NEW YORK
2011

For information about permission to reproduce selections from this book,
write to Permissions, Houghton Mifflin Harcourt Publishing Company,
215 Park Avenue South, New York, New York 10003.

www.hmhbooks.com

Library of Congress Cataloging-in-Publication Data
Phinney, Davis.
The happiness of pursuit : a father's courage, a son's love, and life's
steepest climb / Davis Phinney, Austin Murphy.
p. cm.
ISBN 978-0-547-31593-5 (hardback)
1. Phinney, Davis. 2. Cyclists — United States — Biography. 3. Parkinson's
disease — Patients — United States — Biography. 4. Fathers and sons —
United States. I. Murphy, Austin. II. Title.
GV1051.P52A3 2011
796.6092 — dc22
[B]   2010049820

Book design by Melissa Lotfy

Printed in the United States of America

DOC 10 9 8 7 6 5 4 3 2 1

This book is dedicated to my family.

Contents

Introduction

I DIDN'T KNOW WHERE the kid was going. I just knew it was going to be interesting. I was standing next to my twenty-year-old son Taylor on the dais at an awards banquet in Davis, California. I'd just introduced him to a crowd of three hundred or so people at a ceremony hosted by the US Bicycling Hall of Fame. USA Cycling had named Taylor its 2010 Male Athlete of the Year.

As he made his way to the lectern, someone fired up a Lady Gaga tune, inspiring T to shake his booty in the direction of the crowd, which roared with laughter. The prospect of giving an acceptance speech didn't exactly rattle him.

Taylor could have talked about any number of victories: in the five years he's been racing a bike, he's won five world championships. Instead, he told the story of "the Text," a message I'd sent him as he struggled through a tough French race called the Tour de l'Avenir. After winning the prologue — a short, solo effort against the clock — he'd crashed heavily on a rain-slicked descent toward the end of the second stage. As he lay dazed and bleeding on the road, his shorts and jersey shredded, he was ringed by anxious onlookers: his team director, Patrick Jonker, and several paramedics, all of them Tour de France veterans. They urged him to abandon the race, to board the waiting ambulance. Shaking them off, T climbed back on his bike. He went from the yellow jersey to the *lanterne rouge* that day — from first to last. After returning from the hospital with a half mile of bandages on his left side, he took the start the next morning.

He raced in pain that day and the next. On the eve of Stage 5, the most mountainous and difficult of the race, he sent me a text, describing his condition as "pretty f-ed." His will to keep racing seemed to be wavering. "If they go crazy on those climbs tomrw and I get dropped . . . not sure if I'll finish."

"So I send that to my dad," Taylor told his audience, "and I get back a text about *this* long." He held his thumb and forefinger about five inches apart.

While laughing along with the crowd, I also reflected on how much time it had taken me to peck out a five-inch text message. Since my diagnosis with young-onset Parkinson's disease about ten years ago, my hands don't work as well as they used to.

Taylor wanted to bail on the race, is what it boiled down to, and he wanted my blessing. Which was not forthcoming.

"Hmmm. OK. See how it goes," is how I began my reply. "Start with the mindframe that you're gonna finish the stage, tho, otherwise you're done for sure." And I proceeded to lay it on thick. If he was capable of competing, he needed to honor his commitment to his team, to show his true character, to remember what his mother and I had instilled in him from the beginning, the lesson my own father had drilled into me: *Phinneys don't quit.*

Before beginning this memoir, I held in my head a CliffsNotes version of my father as a kind of cold, close-minded scientist who impeded my success as much as he enabled it. The exercise of writing this book made me realize, fairly quickly, that while it made my journey seem slightly more heroic — *Look at everything I've had to overcome!* — the CliffsNotes version was incomplete, and unfair.

Damon Dodge Phinney had more depth and generosity than I long gave him credit for. His love was often disguised, but always present. Even as he disagreed with what he viewed as my risky, wrong-headed career choice, he supported me. In his way. He took time off from his job to drive me to races from Kentucky to Canada to California. His fervent wish that I *wasn't* racing didn't stop him from peppering me with advice on how to *race better*. One or two days after my competitions, he would slide unsolicited, single-spaced typed letters under my apartment door. Disapproving of my line of work (he would have much preferred to see me head off to college) didn't preclude him from holding — and sharing — strong opinions on how I went about my job. After giving them a brisk once-over, I usually tossed them, believing I knew better. As I grew older and recalled his advice, I was struck by how spot-on and incisive it often was.

Damon was diagnosed with metastatic prostate cancer in 1987. It was grim news, and, in its way, a blessing. Rather than a death sentence, he heard a gong that jarred him out of his lifelong stoicism. It was in the final fourteen years of his life that my father truly learned to reach out to people, to show the world his inner light, even as he fought his cancer like a Spartan at Thermopylae. In so doing, he set an example of grace and courage that turned out to be his greatest gift to me, as I cope with my own chronic disease.

"Phinneys don't quit," declared Taylor, explaining to the audience why he gutted it out in Stage 5 at the Tour de l'Avenir. Because he made that decision, because he pushed through the pain, because he *endured*, he learned something vital. T stayed the course, worked hard for his team, and, following that ebb, he began to flow. He felt stronger at the end of that eight-day race than he had in the beginning. And the form he found in the final stages of L'Avenir helped him ten days later in Greenville, South Carolina.

There, he won his first professional national road title, eking out a 0.14-second victory over Levi Leipheimer in the USPRO time trial championships — a stunning outcome. Levi is one of the best in the world in that discipline. A fortnight after Greenville, Taylor won the U23 (under twenty-three) world title in the same event in Melbourne, Australia.

Those races down under were his last as an *espoir*. (That's a French word for a promising young rider. Translated literally, it means "hope.") T was primed for his next quantum leap — this time to the top of the pro ranks. He'd recently signed a multimillion-dollar deal with the BMC professional racing team. Funded by Swiss businessman Andy Rihs, BMC is directed by my old boss, Jim Ochowicz.

It was Och (rhymes with "coach") who created the 7-Eleven team I rode with for nine years, from its early-'80s success in this country through its pioneering days as the first North American team to contest the Tour de France. Twenty years after my last race in the red, white, and green tricot of Team Slurpee, as we were known, we entrusted Taylor to Jim's care.

To follow Taylor's races in Melbourne, I found myself devouring Twitter updates at 3 A.M. in a Glasgow hotel. While he was in Australia for Worlds, I was in Scotland for the World Parkinson's Congress. In addition to serving as a featured speaker at three of the sessions, I represented the foundation that bears my name. Meeting with leaders in the PD community, I engaged in our ongoing conversation on how to live better with this disease.

Sixteen years after I stopped riding a bike for a living, I'm still in a race. But this is a race I can't quit, or even take a break from. Like an insidious vine, Parkinson's has crept and coiled its way into every corner and recess of my life, slowing me in all ways. The disease has forced me to see the world differently — to recognize and seize the small moments, the hidden grace notes available to us every day. That explains the tag line, or motto, of the Davis Phinney Foundation: Every Victory Counts.

Three of Taylor's world titles, incidentally, have come in the individual pursuit, an event contested by riders who start on opposite sides of a banked oval track. *The Happiness of Pursuit* is more than just a pun on my son's track specialty. On a deeper level, "pursuit" denotes action. It is the opposite of the inertia and resignation that have settled on too many members of my tribe, as I refer to my tremulous collective. "Pursuit" in this context means taking responsibility for your own happiness. It is the pro-active seeking out of what I have come to call "curative moments."

Living the last two decades with PD, I've learned to savor and magnify these moments. I appreciate that I have more control over the course of the disease than I once thought, and that these lesser triumphs provide their own source of cure. And that is the heart, the crux, the essence of my message to the tribe.

With a chronic illness, it can be all too easy to live in the shadows, to become absorbed in the down times, but in bike racing, as in life, it's imperative never to *renoncer a l'espoir* — to give up hope. To concede, to abandon the race, is to miss out on those charged instances, those gratifying moments of victory, those few seconds that sustain us. Those stories, and the lessons therein, make up the happiness of pursuit.

THE HAPPINESS OF PURSUIT

1

— — —

Good News

GIVE ME ROLLING country roads through Loire Valley farmland or the vineyards of the Piedmont. Give me a circuit race around my hometown of Boulder, Colorado, or a boiling field sprint down the main drag of Anytown, Anywhere. God help me in the mountains.

Such was my mindset during the two decades I raced a bike for a living. In the animal kingdom of pro road cycling, I fell into the phylum of Sprinter — that impatient, impetuous, not-quite-sane breed of biker transforming the final meters of many races into a kind of seething velo-riot. I lived for those moments — for the danger, the surge of adrenaline; for the chance to prove, on good days, that I was the fastest cat in the jungle. And I had a lot of good days.

But the same oversized muscle groups that kept me up front in a bunch sprint tended to weigh me down when the road rose. I didn't contest the mountain stages so much as I survived them.

Why is it, then, nearly two decades after my last race, that my thoughts so often return to the Alps, the Pyrenees, the jagged spires of the Dolomites? Why, upon returning to Europe, do I seek out the old, familiar giants — the Stelvio and the Gavia, the Col d'Aubisque and Croix de Fer — that kicked my butt back in the day?

Because of their unmatched beauty—a majesty magnified, in my mind, by the price one pays to drink it in. Because the act of grinding up some mile-high beast serves, in its way, as a stripped-down metaphor for life. The process is at once painful and rewarding, beautiful and, well, *uphill.* We are awestruck by nature and humbled by our tiny place in it. It hurts, and we keep going.

I won hundreds of races in my career, but I found out more about myself on the days I struggled. Let me begin this book, in that case, with the story of one of my toughest days in the saddle, the day I came in almost dead last in a stage of the Tour de France.

I wasn't supposed to be at that Tour in the first place. I was supposed to be at my wife's side, supporting her and making the acquaintance of our newborn son. Seven years after we were married, six years after the Olympics, five years after I turned pro, three years after we'd started trying to conceive a child, in the small hours of June 27, 1990, Connie went into labor with Taylor, whose due date wasn't for another two weeks. Having moved up the timetable, Taylor then decided that, on second thought, he was in no hurry to leave the womb. Positioned posterior (the back of his head toward Connie's back), he basically got stuck in the birth canal and had to be yanked into the light by our burly, forceps-wielding obstetrician, Dr. Robert Macsalka.

Mother and son emerged from the ordeal a tad the worse for wear: she in need of stitches, he looking bruised and a bit, well, *squished.* We hadn't yet settled on a name for a boy.

"Let's call him Stephen!" I blurted out of the blue.

Connie iced me with her eyes. If you know her, you know the look I'm talking about. "Stephen? We never, ever discussed Stephen." So much for Stephen.

Connie was far more receptive, ironically, when I made a far less reasonable request. After phoning the glad tidings to various members of our families, I placed a call to my friend and boss, Jim Ochowicz, director of 7-Eleven, my team for the previous eight years. Och was overjoyed for us, and dutifully jotted down Taylor's vital statistics — one of which he took the liberty of rounding down in the ensuing press release. Taylor's birth weight was seven pounds, twelve ounces. Donning his publicist's cap, Och announced to the world that the lad had checked in — Oh, the serendipity! — at seven pounds, eleven ounces. Get it? Seven eleven.

Before I hung up, he hit me with a thunderbolt: "Do you want to come ride the Tour? We could use you."

It was a rhetorical question, really. If you're a pro baseball player, you want to pitch in the World Series. I was a pro cyclist — of *course* I wanted to ride the Tour. I'd raced three Tours for 7-Eleven. But with Connie scheduled to pop during the 1990 Tour de France, I'd put in for paternity leave. Och had been cool about it. I'd entered some shorter, domestic races, and generally stayed closer to home.

Now, three days before the start of the Tour, Och was inviting me to come pitch in the World Series, basically. Standing there in the hospital lobby, my heart started racing. The debate in my head didn't last very long.

"HELL YEAH I'll ride the Tour," I replied. "I'll be over there in a Tag Heuer minute. But, uh, first let me clear it with Connie."

She was still flushed with exhaustion, still radiant with the afterglow of childbirth — it was either that or the anesthetic hadn't yet worn off — when I gingerly broached the subject.

"The Tour? Now?"

Well, not now, not exactly. I wouldn't fly to France until *tomorrow*, I explained. As a sprinter, I assured her, my primary role would be over after the first week or so. Och said I would probably be home in ten days, tops. I was being at least a little disingenuous: the Tour is cycling's grandest stage, and no pro ever starts it with the idea that he won't finish. Not even me, not even that summer, when I wasn't physically prepared to get through all twenty-one of its stages.

Despite the short notice and a chaotic interval of packing and preparing, I was eager to test myself. The first week of the Tour would cover the windswept, northern end of France. Those were stages that typically ended in a field sprint, my specialty.

In her stupor, and never having managed a newborn before, Connie acquiesced. I could swear she said, "For your love of the sport, for your commitment to your job, to honor who you are at your core, go to France." More likely, her response was along the lines of, "Uh, yeah, I guess so."

Which is how I found myself, three days later, at a French theme park called Futuroscope, rolling down the ramp for the prologue of the 77th Tour de France.

The *Grand Boucle,* or Big Loop, as the French refer to their Super Bowl, is a terrible beauty, a three-week celebration of suffering that averages more than a hundred miles a day, raced at a merciless pace, over a wide variety of terrain. The 1990 Tour covered 2,174 miles, our average speed nearly twenty-five miles an hour.

In other years, I might've been able to spend more time out of the wind, conserving energy, poaching a few field sprints while riding myself into Tour shape. As luck would have it, Steve Bauer, a longtime friend, formal rival, and now my 7-Eleven teammate, captured the yellow leader's jersey on the very first stage. We, the members of Team Slurpee, as we were known back in the States, assumed the responsibility for defending the *maillot jaune.* Instead of trying to set myself up for sprint wins, I was thrust into the role of protector. All of us were. It was honorable, all-consuming, hard work.

For the next eight days, as the course swept us north to Normandy, east toward the German border, then south to the Alps, it was all hands on deck. My teammates and I spent about fourteen hundred kilometers riding hard tempo on the front, our noses in the wind, chasing down breaks, defending the jersey. We were cooked at the end of every stage. And we were thrilled. *We were leading the Tour de France!* I say "we" because the teamwork in road cycling, while not as overt as in baseball or basketball, is a critical part of the sport. Turning ourselves inside out for Steve every day was just one example. That all-for-one ethic was another thing making it so difficult for me to pull out of the '90 Tour after just a week or so. What if Steve needed help at a crucial moment and I wasn't there to give it to him?

As the race passed its tenth day and entered the Alps, I suffered more profoundly. I was fried from defending the jersey, and now we were headed into the unwelcoming (to me) terrain of the mountains. Stage 11 took us over a trio of legendary cols, or passes. As soon as the road so much as slightly tilted up to the base of the Col de la Madeleine — a sweet-sounding name for a bitch of a climb — it felt like someone had stolen my legs and replaced them with a cadaver's. Seriously, the peloton whooshed past me as if I were running an errand on a fat-tired cruiser bike. Gasping and struggling against the grade and my fatigue, I progressively lost time, so much so that, gazing up the mountain at one point, I caught sight of the main pack as it reached the summit. I was almost two miles behind.

Cresting the climb, I found myself twenty minutes in arrears, and the stark truth dawned on me: my race was over. Making a quick calculation, I figured the time limit to be around forty to forty-five minutes. (Riders who fail to finish a stage within a certain percentage of the winner's time are unceremoniously booted from the race.) I'd lost half that in just twenty-five kilometers, and had another hundred clicks, and two major mountain passes, to go!

Although the notion of quitting was anathema to me, the thoughts came crowding in: I didn't *need* to keep suffering. I was free to hit the eject button any time. *You've done your job,* I reasoned. *Let it go. Nobody expected you to even get this far.* I had a newborn son back home, awaiting my return. Relaxing, if not quite surrendering, I drifted down the descent, actually enjoying the view.

At the base of the next climb was a feed zone, where a team car awaited. I visualized the process; rolling to the side of the road and dismounting, I would stand as the race commissaire unpinned my race number. Like Chuck Connors having his epaulets torn off at the beginning of each episode of *Branded,* I would endure that brief, unpleasant ritual, and then it would be over.

I couldn't see the team car, however, which pissed me off. They couldn't even wait around for me to quit! Just as I got to the end of the zone, a team staffer stepped out with a musette — a feed-bag — for me. I snatched it, out of habit more than anything — and kept right on riding. The voice told me I was being an idiot: *What are you doing?* I thought. *Turn around.* But quitting simply felt wrong. Instead, I wolfed down a panino, or small sandwich, drank a can of Coke, and started the next climb. From somewhere, I found a rhythm and began to feel human again.

Working my way up the lower slopes of the Col du Glandon, I had a kind of epiphany. Maybe, I reasoned, everything I'd ever learned on the bike, every day I'd been on the road — all the training, all the racing, all the suffering — had led me to this day, this ride, this moment. And Just. Like. That. I had my mission.

Self-serving? To be sure. But for reasons I can't fully explain, it seemed like the decision was made for me — and this would make for one of those life lessons that stick.

Pushing through the switchbacks, I felt myself gaining strength. Up ahead, I sighted another racer, a Spanish rider, fighting for survival like me. An ally! Slowly, I worked my way up to him, knowing that our chances would be improved riding together. I was almost smiling. At the summit, just as I swept ahead and motioned for him to get in my draft, my compadre blew a tire, and I never saw him again.

Quick regroup. More self-talk: *Remember your mission!*

I've never smoked a descent the way I did going down the back

side of the Glandon that day. Mimicking a skier's tuck—arms
and knees pulled inward, chin an inch off the handlebars—I was
pushing sixty-five miles an hour on the narrow, bumpy tarmac.
Fully aware of the danger, I had to continually fight the urge to
brake. But I was all-in. In the flow. And it felt good. The clock was
ticking.

Still to come: the notorious twenty-one switchbacks of the Alpe
d'Huez. The serpentine road gains more than three thousand feet
in less than ten miles to finish at a ski station. It's not the steepest
climb of the Tour, nor is it the highest, nor the most beautiful. It is
simply the most infamous, arriving, usually, at the end of an epic
(read: brutal) stage. Like this one. An hour's drive from Grenoble,
it always draws huge crowds. On this day, there were a half million
people on the mountain, most of them making their way down
as I approached her flanks, way behind the leaders. Rather than
mock my late arrival, they applauded and encouraged me. Understanding the stakes, they saluted my effort.

Allez! Allez! Hop, hop! Dai, dai, dai!
Courage, Phinney! (Cou-RAHJ Fee-NAY! is how it sounded.)

Their languages and cheers flowed together, willing me forward. So thick were the crowds, I found myself in a vortex of noise
and sweat and energy. Plenty of those fans had camped out; they'd
been partying for days. It was a raucous, unruly group, so I was
gratified to see a motorcycle gendarme tuck in ahead of me ten
switchbacks from the top, to lead me through the chaos. I ate his
fumes the whole way, the crowd parting just enough for the two of
us to get past. Any pain I might have felt was smothered by deaf-
ening noise and a sea of energy as hands reached out to push and a
virtual cascade of cooling water was poured continuously over my
head.

Switchbacks done, there remained a slight descent through
town in the final kilometer—last k!—then a hard left with four
hundred meters to go. Later, I learned that Greg LeMond, on his

way to winning his third Tour title, had overshot that turn, allowing the Italian champion Gianni Bugno to take the stage victory.

Sprinting up that finishing straight, I was greeted by the sight
of — F—— me! — a construction crew, already dismantling the
bleachers. They paused to watch as I crossed the line.

I slumped immediately into the arms of Och, who'd stood waiting for me, along with team PR liaison Sean Petty. I was shattered,
yet oddly at peace. My Tour was over, I felt sure, but I hadn't quit.
I'd given everything. Draping a towel around my shoulders, Jim
said nothing, waiting for me to compose myself before he whis-
pered, finally, "Two minutes. You made it by two minutes."

I had made it. A week later I would ride past my parents, who'd
flown from Colorado for the final week of the race, never having
seen me in the Tour before. And when my son finally came of age,
I would share with him what I learned on that epic day.

Twenty years later, I still draw on the lessons of July 11, 1990.
I had no way of knowing, then, that I would call on that experience so often in the decades that followed — not to improve my
athletic performance, but as a tool to cope with this gathering in-
firmity. During my darkest moments, when I'm struggling not just
to speak, but to think clearly; when it's a challenge to get food to
my mouth, when I'm shuffling and stumbling and hard-pressed to
come up with a single positive "moment" for my end-of-the-day
inventory, I think back to that Alpine stage, the day I damn near
came in last, but won.

I reflect on the need to get past one's self-pity during those inevitable low moments; of setting goals, then fighting for them, no
matter the odds.

That long day on the Alpe proved a triumph — if only to me. In
losing I gained something so valuable that it shines like a beacon
within me. I know I can persevere. I can do this. While I may en-
tertain occasional thoughts about quitting, I am not a quitter. I will

not give a millimeter to this disease, will not let it take me easily. I will pursue life, pursue *living,* with grace and guts.

Of course I want to live to see a cure for my disease — and to make that time limit, too. But until that glad day arrives, I want to live well, not merely exist.

I want to emphasize the importance of hanging in there, fighting the good fight, not quitting. Don't give up hope. If you can keep your focus and hang on until the *next* mountain, the *next* switchback, the *next* finish line, there might just be a friend waiting for you with a dry towel and a bit of good news.

2

--- --- ---

Diagnosis

I N MARCH OF 2000 I found myself in the foothills of Australia's Snowy Mountains, doing color commentary on a women's
bike race called (what else?) the Tour de Snowy. Six weeks after
that, I planned to be in Europe, serving as primary commentator
for the Outdoor Life Network's coverage of the Giro d'Italia (Tour
of Italy). Before I went down under, I celebrated the International
Cycling Union's centenary ride from Paris to Geneva with some
of the greats in cycling history. That is a capsule of my postrac-
ing life.

As a cycling commentator, I was living the dream. The transition to television had gone smoothly for me. I knew the sport, the
riders, the directors. And I was comfortable in front of the camera—as any of my ex-teammates would be happy to tell you. Indeed, they might go so far as to say I never saw a live mike I didn't
love.

"Davis was a fantastic ambassador for the sport," my former
7-Eleven teammate Bob Roll once told a reporter. "He had broad
perspective and great grasp of its selling points."

What I had was a master plan. I was laying the groundwork for
my career off the bike. Aside from the on-air assignments, I inhab-

ited the role of sports marketing director for Pearl Izumi, a Colorado-based cycling and athletic-apparel company that Connie and I helped get off the ground in the late 1980s by buying a piece of it. In that capacity I'd signed a deal with the US Postal Service cycling team that had seen American phenom Lance Armstrong win his first Tour de France title, in Pearl Izumi clothing, in 1999. As was my habit, I was covering a lot of bases, saying yes to virtually every opportunity. I delighted in coaching Taylor's soccer team, wrote columns for various cycling publications, crisscrossed the country giving clinics and motivational speeches. Connie and I hosted our annual Bike Camps, which we'd begun in 1986. We also wrote a book, *Training for Cycling: The Ultimate Guide to Improved Performance.*

Producers saw potential in me, and I ended up getting as much work as I could handle, doing commentary for NBC, CBS, ABC, and ESPN. When the Outdoor Life Network (OLN, now Versus) launched in 1995, I was one of its first hires. At the Tour de Snowy five years later, I was doing a prerace interview with Karen Kurreck, a former world time-trial champion. As Karen and I bantered about the scorching heat and her crash in Stage 2, I noticed—Karen noticed, everyone noticed, you couldn't *help* but notice—that my left hand, which held the microphone, was shaking uncontrollably. I had to focus every fiber of my being on holding that mike steady, just to get through the interview. Afterward, the Australian camerawoman working with me said, "JAY-zus, Davis, eets hot as an oven out here. Why're you shivering?"

I don't know, I sheepishly told her. Maybe I'd had too much coffee. Deep down, though, I knew I had a bigger problem: weakness and tingling in my left arm; a constant dead feeling in my left leg; cramping in my foot; tripping. The odd fact that I didn't swing my left arm when I ran. On hikes, Connie would note that my gait seemed stilted, that I seemed to be walking in slow motion, with smaller, mincing steps.

Something was clearly out of whack in my body, but with my "exercise junkie" mentality and post–cycling career work schedule, there always seemed to be some rational explanation. From my racing days, I'd grown accustomed to the usual buffet of aches, pains, fatigue, and miscellaneous discomforts. So I thought little of this grab bag of disparate symptoms. The deep, chronic fatigue that had plagued me, on and off, for a decade could always be explained away. To fend it off, I'd get myself a massage or a chiropractic adjustment or dabble in various nutritional supplements. As the months and years went past, these remedies proved less and less effective at warding off the shroud closing in around me. It made me happy, but probably didn't improve my health, that I was now fully—almost obsessively—indulging my cold-weather passion for cross-country skiing. I ended up training hard, year-round. Unlike my bike-racing days, where rest and recovery were built into my schedule, I now left myself little chance to recover.

Of course, Connie and I were overscheduled, but so were most of the other parents of young children we knew. (Three and a half years after Taylor was born, we'd welcomed our beautiful daughter, Kelsey, into the world.) *You're always tired?* I would think to myself. *Well, take a number.* Often, I'd hit some invisible limit, then find myself running a fever that would force me to bed for a day or two. Thinking back on those recurrent fevers, I wonder if my body wasn't trying to fight off the disease; surely it was trying to get my attention. I was hearing it, obviously, but I wasn't *listening.*

My tremoring hand, finally, at the Tour de Snowy, was a clarion call that sounded louder than all of those other symptoms. It scared me on a deeper level. Upon my return to Boulder, Connie noticed it right away. "Wow—look at that!" she'd say as the coffee sloshed back and forth in the mug I was holding. Even then I was still rationalizing: perhaps my hand shook because of nerve damage from slicing open my forearm in a bad crash years before in Belgium. That, of course, would not have explained the fatigue, the frequent tripping, the lack of swing in my left arm.

What followed was an exasperating, months-long mission to find out what the hell the problem was. I saw a series of doctors and specialists, none of whom diagnosed me correctly. It was a deeply frustrating period during which it felt, to me, as if the docs were throwing darts at a board. After several CAT scans and numerous MRIs, I joked—although the experience was pretty far from funny—about becoming a member of the Frequent Fryer Club (a decade later, I can still hear the jackhammering from those claustrophobic sessions in the MRI chamber).

Keeping in contact with me throughout this period was Dr. Andy Pruitt, an old friend, and the founder of the Boulder Center for Sports Medicine. Andy had a good grasp on my medical history. We discovered that, the day I'd ridden into the rear window of a team car during a 1988 race called Liège-Bastogne-Liège, I'd also fractured the C1 vertebra in my neck, an injury that went undiagnosed at the time. I reasoned that the tingling and shaking in my left hand could be tied to that long-ago spill.

Andy recognized that there was something more profoundly wrong with me. While an old neck injury might explain some of the issues on my left side, it didn't account for the tremoring. Shannon Browning, the wife of my longtime friend and training partner Ray Browning, worked in Boulder as a PT, specializing in head trauma. She took a look at me and grasped after just a brief evaluation that these disparate symptoms were all originating in my brain. The old neck injury, she believed, was a red herring, throwing us off the track.

Finally, Andy directed us to a respected Denver neurologist—a movement-disorder specialist who was on the brink of retirement. He agreed to see me on short notice, and put me through a battery of tests: He gauged the strength of my left arm relative to that of my right. He checked the flexibility of my joints. He tapped my knees with a mallet, noting the disparity in reactions between left and right. He inspected my handwriting. Finally, he wrote me a prescription for a pill called Sinemet, which boosts dopamine levels in the brain. Dopamine is a neurotransmitter that helps regulate the body's movement.

"Try this and see if it works," he told me.

The good news was that I responded immediately to the Sinemet. I spoke more clearly, wrote with greater ease—I'm left-handed—and walked more gracefully. Right away I was stronger on the bike. Where I'd begun to feel lopsided, weak on my left side, all of a sudden I was my old self, powering up mountains in a big gear.

The bad news was that Sinemet, a commercial form of levodopa, is the gold standard of tests for a major disorder of the central nervous system. If you respond really well to it, in effect, you've tested positive. As the neurologist put it to me on my return visit: "Young man, I'm sorry to be the one to have to tell you this, but I believe you have Parkinson's disease."

I was forty years old.

By that point, I wasn't completely shocked by the diagnosis. Before I took the Sinemet, Connie had shared with me, and with the neurologist, her suspicion that I suffered from Parkinson's, a suspicion that the neurologist shared. Between appointments, I'd found a website on young-onset Parkinson's and taken the ten-symptom quiz I found there. It asked questions like: Are you tremoring? Are you experiencing rigidity? Having problems with balance? Having problems with your gait? Uh, yeah. Yep. Check. I suspected I was in trouble after acing that test.

But there was a stark finality to the actual diagnosis; I still remember sitting in the office of the neurologist, a man in the twilight of his career, realizing that an important part of my life was at an end as well. It was a surreal feeling—as if I was a third-party witness to a kind of sentencing, as if I was observing some sap get really shitty news and thinking, *Oh, man, that poor guy—sucks for him,* and then having it hit me. *Holy shit, that guy is ME! How am I going to handle this?*

I'd like to report that I handled the diagnosis with calm and equanimity, that after sharing an embrace with Connie, we began mapping out a plan for coping with this setback in our lives. The truth is, we drove back to Boulder in relative silence and stopped at Zolo's, a Boulder restaurant, where I sat at the bar and threw back several shots of tequila. I've never been much of a drinker. But I needed to check out—if only for that evening.

I called my bosses at OLN and delivered the bad news, telling them I was out for the Giro. They knew, and I knew, that my television career was probably over, although no one was saying it at the time. Parkinson's disease affects the voice, and for me, a storyteller gifted with sound effects and accents, it would be a struggle to maintain normal speech, much less emote or mimic as I had once done. For all its ravages, PD would help me realize, eventually, that I was put on earth to do something more important than win bike races and talk about them on TV. But in the spring of 2000, those redeeming rays were not visible from the cave into which I was only now beginning to descend. Nor would they be for many months.

What causes Parkinson's? Scientists believe it's a combination of genetics and environment. You've got a better chance of developing PD if you live in a rural community, drink well water, or have been exposed to pesticides. It's interesting to note that Parkinson's was documented only after the Industrial Revolution—which unleashed a dramatically increased level of environmental toxins on the world. Why one person gets Parkinson's and another doesn't is poorly understood. Right now, there are between 1 million and 1.5 million Americans with the disease, around 5 million worldwide. PD is primarily diagnosed in people over the age of sixty; I was one of the 5 to 10 percent of PD cases that occur in people under the age of forty.

I am descended from a long line of rational, pragmatic engineers. Introspection was never a strong suit in my family, which is why I've never spent much time mulling over the question Why me? That said . . . *Why me?*

I personally believe that I carry a genetic predisposition for PD that was exacerbated by my chosen profession, which was basically to torture my body to its outermost limits for twenty years, causing vast quantities of free-radical damage — damage that perhaps my particular genetic code wasn't prepared to handle. I also carry the PARK2 gene, which is thought to play a role in young-onset PD, the result of various mutations involving protein accumulation. I don't know what percentage of the population may also carry that gene, nor do I know what percentage of people within that population will develop PD. I do know that the blows I took to the head both before I was cycling (I was hit by cars multiple times crossing the street when I was a kid) and during my cycling career, combined with the extreme conditions under which I raced, almost certainly contributed.

Trying to buck me up not long after I was diagnosed, Och asked, "Are you sure the doctors are right? You look pretty good to me." He meant well, but that compliment didn't exactly help. Yes, I still presented well. That didn't mean my world hadn't been turned upside down. But throughout, I've managed to stay fit and lean. My outward appearance is usually pretty good, which works against me sometimes.

Three weeks after I got my bad news, Connie's older brother Chuck was diagnosed with metastasized lymphoma. After picking themselves off the floor, he and his family formed a battle plan. Neighbors and loved ones rallied to their side, signing up to prepare their meals throughout his chemo and radiation. Cancer is something you fight, an identifiable opponent that requires a tactical battle plan. PD is much tougher to target, a band of guerrilla fighters who melt into the countryside. And the more profound difference is that with cancer—and luckily, in Chuck's case—you can be cured. No such hope exists for PD at the moment. After my diagnosis, I didn't brace myself for a heroic clash with my disease. There is no known cure for PD, so there was no showdown with it, no course of chemo to gird for, nothing to rally around. You sit around; the phone doesn't ring. Friends were unsure how to react, or what to say, so they said nothing. Well-intentioned people, who were unfamiliar with the disease, would blurt out things like, "my [fill in the blank—brother, cousin, babysitter, etc.] had something like that once, but it got better. You'll be fine." Well, not exactly. But thanks for the concern. They didn't get it. PD isn't like catching a cold. My second neurologist told us with great assurance that he would have me feeling as good as I've ever felt—for years to come. Hopeful sentiment? More like a lie if I'd ever heard one.

I'm not saying my brain wasn't hitting on all cylinders in that first year after my diagnosis, when I was popping a smorgasbord of pills, struggling to figure out which ones worked best for me. But that was around the time I concluded that the one thing that could make me truly happy was the purchase of a sports car. Big smile. Anyone for a Porsche?

I called my go-to guy for impulsive toy procurement, Rick Beswick, in California, who quickly had a line on a 1995 Porsche 993, one of the last of the air-cooled models. It had custom wheels, was in terrific shape. The owner was asking $40K. "Sold," I said. I mean, it was *important* that I have this car.

At the time, Och was managing some of our money. I told him I needed him to sell some stock to free up some cash. He seemed a bit surprised, but followed instructions. Just before I pulled the trigger, I mentioned to Connie, in as casual a tone as I could manage, that I was about to launch on a seriously cool Porsche. Somehow I'd gotten that far along without discussing the subject with her. The exchange did not go in my favor.

"What the—how much is it?"

"Forty thousand, but it's worth every—"

"FORTY THOUSAND? Are you KIDDING? Is this disease affecting your JUDGMENT?"

After she'd calmed down, Connie made the point that I'd just quit several jobs, and that dropping serious coin on a sports car might not be the most prudent move at this time in our lives. Damn. Called Rick back to cancel the buy and headed back to Zolo's.

What she didn't take into account was the fact that PD *does* affect your judgment. Maybe not the disease itself, but the medications one takes to control it. I definitely was not myself, but in truth I didn't know who "myself" was anymore. I was lost.

Speaking with a friend of ours, Dr. Max Testa, Connie confided that I seemed unmoored, disoriented, a bit of a stranger. "It will probably take him two years to reinvent himself," he told her. It was encouraging to hear that I might eventually pull out of this nosedive. First I had to finish descending.

This was not too long after actor Michael J. Fox had gone public with Parkinson's, a disease he'd lived with and managed silently while maintaining a thriving career. Michael was the poster child for young-onset PD. While most of the general public associates PD with people of their grandparents' age, he paved the way for those like me (and, like Lance Armstrong, would start a highly successful foundation in his name, a road I would eventually take, too).

Fox shocked many of his fans in 1999 when he appeared before a Senate subcommittee holding hearings on Parkinson's research, without first having taken his PD meds. The urgency felt by the Parkinson's community, he later explained in a 2003 memoir, "demanded that my testimony about the effects of the disease . . . be seen as well as heard. For people who had never observed me in this kind of shape, the transformation must have been startling."

His early advocacy helped my cause. It enabled me to say, "You know what Michael J. Fox has — that's my disease."

But it was a grim interval in my life. I had zero desire to be viewed as a victim, and so desperately wanted to hide my symptoms — even as I was becoming more symptomatic. That Denver doctor who was viewed as a "guru" in the treatment of PD — the guy who'd assured me, "You're gonna feel as good as you've ever felt!" — was basically full of shit. Which is what I felt like at the time.

I went to other doctors, who prescribed various cocktails of pills. But the meds just made a mess of me, wreaking havoc on mind and body alike. For six months I was a zombie, fighting off narcolepsy, depression, and a bewildering, general chemical-induced haze. The overall sensation was of a man being sucked slowly under. Under what? — under water? It felt more like quicksand. Parkinson's encased me. I felt incarcerated in my own body.

By the time most people are diagnosed with PD, they've lost significant amounts of dopamine-producing cells. So their personalities are changing even *before* they fill their prescriptions for pills. Those pills often do an OK job of reducing base symptoms, but they can also scramble body chemistry, further altering personality. Between that drug-induced disequilibrium and the anxiety and self-consciousness brought on by worsening symptoms, I found myself losing my grasp on my own identity, my sense of myself. I was becoming a different person, or at least a different version of the same person.

I visited a neuropsych doc who put me through a battery of tests aimed at providing us with a baseline. I was interested and saddened, but not in the least bit *surprised,* to learn that my brain function correlated closely to what was going on in my body. As I fatigued, my cognition essentially froze up. I became, in a sense, stupid.

On the upside, when I was fresh, I had excellent mental acuity. I took some solace in that, but I slowly came to realize that in fact the brain is the last frontier of science and very poorly understood. So while we could try to measure parameters and experiment with various meds, the reality was that while the prescribed cocktail might work for one, it was, in most cases, definitely *not* working for me. With my family's support, I would have to find my own way.

My wife and children also found themselves forced to navigate uncharted waters. While the changes in me undoubtedly rocked her world, Connie possessed both the temperament and training to hold things together during a family crisis. She'd grown up in the shadow of chronic, debilitating disease: her mother suffered from multiple sclerosis. Darcy Carpenter handled her affliction with poise and grace and wit, and proved a great example for me. Connie's father, Charlie, committed so completely to supporting his wife that his career took a back seat. "I lost my ambition," he said once, in a moment of extreme candor, "when Darcy was diagnosed with MS." Connie and I had no way of knowing the depth of the sacrifices she would have to make, for me. It turned out, they were not small.

Taylor was just ten when I was diagnosed, while Kels was six. What it meant for them at the time was that, quite suddenly, I was home. Full time. I prided myself on being an involved and active parent, but in the weeks and months after my diagnosis I was definitely not 100 percent available. After years of being on the road more than one hundred days per year, I was finally home. I just wasn't at home in my body. Who was I? I felt like a shell.

Children are amazingly adaptable, but they are most happy in a safe and loving environment. This is what we tried our best to give them before and after the diagnosis. We also spared them the details they didn't need to know, given their age. We gave it to them straight, but appropriately filtered, while keeping the focus on them. Kids are naturally egocentric; the world revolves around them. Most difficult perhaps for them were the reactions of other adults. We counseled them frequently about why people responded the way they did. Harder, maybe, was trying to prove to them that my illness wasn't a tragedy, when deep down, it sure felt like one.

3

———

The Road

PARKINSON'S ARRIVED ON my doorstep with ill news, yes — but also bearing gifts. It imposed on me a profound attitude adjustment, a different way of looking at the world.

In a sense, PD opened my eyes. Deprived of the old markers by which I'd once measured success, I was wrenched into a different state, an enforced mindfulness. I've grown more aware of — am much better at recognizing and celebrating — the small victories and blessings available to us every day: the sight of the morning sun on the Flatirons, those iconic rock formations outside Boulder; the thoughtfulness of my daughter, reaching for my trembling hand in the airport, to still the shaking; the illicit thrill, every so often, of walking into Amante's café, not far from my house, and ordering one of their killer cupcakes — the kind with the blue frosting — for breakfast.

By savoring and stockpiling and connecting these snapshots, I'm cobbling together my own cure for an incurable disease. Some such moments are fleeting, which is why I've trained myself to be on the lookout for them. Others are so charged with significance, so life changing, that they're impossible to miss.

• • •

We all carry within us a hidden ember, the glow of unrealized potential. I was fourteen when the ember inside me was fanned by a rush of wind—the cyclone spawned by a hundred-plus fast guys whooshing past on their bicycles. I stood transfixed on the side of the street in North Boulder Park, intrigued by this alien carnival of color and sinew and speed.

It was a Sunday afternoon in June 1975. The riders were powering through the final stage of the first-ever Red Zinger Bicycle Classic, named after a popular tea sold by Boulder-based Celestial Seasonings. "The Zinger," later to become the Coors Classic, was a pioneering event that gave many Americans their first taste of Tour de France–style stage racing. And it gave one unmoored adolescent the clearest signal, to that point in his life, of how he might make his way in the world.

In the United States, at the time, and in my eyes, there was something countercultural and exotic about bike racing. There was a dynamic energy, a visceral beauty, a flow to the racing that gobsmacked me. You could literally feel the rush as the peloton ripped past, lap after lap, on that Sunday criterium (a short-course, multilap event). Feeling that breeze, hearing the soundtrack of the race—the rush of wind through spinning spokes, the clicking of gears, snippets of dialogue from within the bunch, the highly caffeinated announcer pumping up (and educating) the crowd—it was intoxicating, irresistible. It felt like the world was talking to me. And I listened.

I was a restless teenager (is that redundant?) in search of an identity, a mold into which to pour the raw power I sensed within myself. I was strong and athletic, at home in my body, in the outdoors. But the ball sports weren't really happening for me. School, for that matter, wasn't really happening for me. And so I made my way around the halls of Boulder High, schlepping my books and a belief that I was in possession of some untapped power, a gift I had no idea how to harness . . . until that day at North Boulder

Park. Watching those guys leave vapor trails, I was hooked, smitten, poleaxed. I rode home — much faster than usual — and delivered the news to my parents: I'm going to be a bike racer!

They might have responded with more enthusiasm if I'd announced that I intended to join the circus. Both of my parents were scientists. Both were avid outdoors people as well — they met on a rock-climbing expedition — but neither knew much about bike racing. Remember, this was before Lance, before Greg Le-Mond, four years before the movie *Breaking Away*, the Oscar-winning coming-of-age story about an Indiana teen obsessed with Italian culture in general and cycling in particular. They only knew that if I chased this dream, it was going to be another distraction from school, another hurdle to my college education.

My parents were far from alone among the skeptics. A year later, I asked my history teacher to please sign a form saying that it was OK for me to miss class for a week to attend a training camp in Texas.

He signed. Reluctantly. And not before making it a point to tell me, "You know, Davis, you'll never make a living in bike racing."

My dad, Damon, bike-commuted to work and still did an annual century (one-hundred-mile) ride. He knew enough about the sport to seriously question whether it held a future for me. Yet he indulged me, suggesting we head out for a "real" ride — twenty-five miles! — to test me out and see how serious I was, I suppose. In those days Dad was riding a venerable but tanklike forty-five-pound Raleigh three-speed that he'd bought back in the '50s, when he was living in Ohio.

I rode the trusty Browning Mach 3 we'd purchased at Arapahoe sports. It was heavy, too, but had ten speeds, most of which I never used, preferring to ride in the biggest gear possible. Damon loaded up his rucksack with canteens and snacks. We rode ten miles east to the town of Louisville, then north past Lafayette. We drank some lemonade out of the canteens, indulged in Dad's

staple outdoor snack — Munster cheese on Triscuits — and admired
the view of the Continental Divide to the west.

I most remember this ride for what happened next. On the
way back to Boulder, after lollygagging (his word) behind him the
whole way, I sprinted past and pushed as hard as I could for the remaining miles. It gave me great satisfaction that Dad couldn't keep
up, couldn't hold my wheel. He was a fit forty-something with
strong endurance — so it made me feel good, gave me a sense of accomplishment, to drop him. Once I got to the Boulder city-limits
sign, I stopped to wait, psyched to receive his impending compliment on my blistering pace. Surely he'd have to acknowledge my
vast potential now! Dad rolled straight past, his face a mask, re-
marking only that I had better learn to ride closer to the right side
of the road.

In the spring of 1995, six years before he died, my father happily
agreed to collaborate on a journal with Jana Blumenthal, a fifth
grader at Whittier Elementary School in Boulder. The journal was
a school project for Jana, whose parents were friends of our family.
The resulting correspondence between this ten-year-old girl and
sixty-seven-year-old grandfather reveals a sensitive, gentle man far
more comfortable sharing his emotions with a near stranger than
he ever had been with my sister or me. Leafing through it nearly a
decade after his death, I'm struck by — and envious of — his generous, intimate tone, his willingness to share confidences and reveal
his innermost thoughts. (*Dear Jana, Gosh, you are a talented person, and it is a delight for me to have you as a journal partner!* . . .
Our journal is full of your artwork, and I love it!)

Where the hell was this guy when I was growing up?

In another entry, Jana posed this rather open-ended question:
What do you think the meaning of life is? "I would ask the question this way," Damon replied: "What is the *purpose* of life?

"We all have talents," he continued, "and we all should try to develop those talents as fully as possible. The more we can do that, the richer our lives, and the lives of those around us, will be."

Again, where was this guy when I was sprawled on the sofa, re-reading dog-eared back issues of *Bike World*? He was the one telling me I was making a big mistake, that I needed a college degree, that if I insisted on pursuing this pipe dream I'd end up working in a bike shop for a few bucks an hour.

He was a good man but, like a lot of guys of his generation, not very skilled at expressing his feelings. A former Army cryptographer with a measured IQ of 150, his job at Ball Aerospace required a seriously elevated security clearance. And the truth is, Damon remained somewhat inscrutable under his own roof.

This emotional stinginess wasn't a willful choice, was not evidence of some underlying meanness. He was simply more comfortable—much, much more comfortable—in his head than he was in the world. I was reminded of that while reading his journal with Jana, who asked him, at one point, if he had been a shy boy.

"I wonder how you happened to pick out that question," he replied, "because it hits the nail so squarely on the head. Yes, for reasons I do not fully understand, but which may be genetic, I was exceptionally shy while I was growing up . . . The child is father of the man, so I remain shy to this day."

Solitary by nature, he burrowed even deeper into himself when I was twelve years old. It was around that time that my mother began a struggle with her mind, and I lost touch with her for a while. All of us did, but my father became a remote presence in his own house.

As the years passed and I started winning races, arriving near the pinnacle of my sport, my parents came to embrace my career choice, and my success led them back, as a couple, to their adventuresome origins, this time through cycling. On a bike tour of the French Alps in the late '80s, Damon and Thea willed their aging bodies up the twenty-one switchbacks of the Alpe d'Huez. After signing the registry at the summit, my mother was informed by an excited Frenchman, "Madame, you are the oldest woman to ride all the way up the Alpe!"

Thea Phinney is eighty-seven as I write this, and could still probably get up the Alpe today. My mother was well ahead of her time, and paid for it. A graduate of Radcliffe, she was a full-time employee at the US Geological Survey. An avid mountaineer, she put healthy, nutritious meals on the table long before the word *organic* gained currency. She is a delight, and I love her, and have always loved her, even when she became something of a stranger to us during the mid-'70s. Some inner turmoil raged within her, causing her emotional spectrum to veer radically from lucid to near madness. It's a condition I can't begin to understand or discuss with her to this day. We lost a lot during that period. Ultimately, I found the bike.

My father's default reaction to this crisis was to draw inward and soldier on. He was not an outwardly demonstrative person to begin with, and I've long wondered if, and to what extent, Mom's condition was triggered, or exacerbated, by his emotional stinginess. With his wife struggling, Damon reacted by . . . pulling back. He started running more, working out at the University of Colorado's Balch Fieldhouse. The man lived among some of the most gorgeous natural scenery in North America but preferred to log his customary six miles on a 220-yard indoor track, compulsively checking his lap splits on the fieldhouse's giant clock.

This is not a woe-is-me appeal. I am establishing how and why it wasn't exactly a heartbreak for me to bail on this particular domestic scene. And bail I did. My coping mechanism was to get out from under that roof as often as possible. Bike racing proved an ideal outlet. It was a solace, a refuge in which I found a second family of like-minded athletes, an excuse to hit the road often and for extended periods of time.

It was during this unsettled time in our household that my parents stopped checking my report cards. I was an apathetic stu-

dent who paid attention to the subjects that interested me. I got by
thanks to my ability to memorize things on short notice, and because I wasn't above flirting with the smart girls, who saved my ass
more than a few times.

My sister was bright and popular and off in her own world. Two
years older than I, Alice knew how to cope. Stay out, stay away. She
was a cheerleader, performed in the drama club, and got all A's.
Our paths seldom crossed, though we were seldom cross with each
other. Without realizing why we were doing it, I'm sure, we both
cultivated support systems outside the less-than-harmonious life
we came to know at 960 Sixth Street.

Oddly, we were a more close-knit family outside that house
than in it. We all loved skiing, both Alpine and Nordic. In the winter, we'd put on our knickers (which identified one as a *real* cross-
country skier), strap on our old-school wooden planks with the
classic three-pin bindings, then go kicking and gliding through the
forest. Sometimes we'd embark on multiday backpacking trips, going from hut to hut in the high mountains.

I enjoyed both downhill and cross-country, but came to favor
the latter. I preferred it, basically, because it required more physical tenacity. It was *harder*. Which suited me. I had a big engine and
was good at it; I was even recruited as a Nordic skier by a handful of colleges and gave it some thought. In the end, cross-country
skiing was a means by which I stayed in shape for cycling. It was a
mistress, and my true love was the bike.

While that made perfect sense to me, it was a tougher sell to
my old man, the Rocket Scientist, who still desperately wanted me
to go to college (from this remove, I can hardly blame him). That
I was so willing to turn up my nose at the offer of a free education
drove him nearly batty.

In fact I was a voracious reader — if the topic interested me. In
those pre–World Wide Web days, I had a tough time finding even
basic information about cycling: how to train, how to take care of

my bike, what comprised good tactics. I scavenged whatever was at hand. By this time my father had been swept up in the "running boom," and based his workouts on the training principles of Arthur Lydiard, a renowned kiwi coach who'd discovered, through trial and error, that his middle-distance runners performed better when they first established a deep, aerobic base. It was left to me to apply Lydiard's concepts to my training on a bicycle. I'd scored a couple of cycling magazines from the Boulder Public Library—*Bike World* and *Bicycling*—which I devoured front to back. I found a secondhand copy of *All About Bike Racing*, rereading its chapters as if they were sacred texts, undeterred by my failure to understand much of its terminology.

Yet my attachment to the sport paled in comparison to the all-consuming obsession of another Boulder-based teenager, a cyclist by the name of Tony Comfort. Waiting nervously to register one morning for one of the first races I ever did, I found myself in line behind a guy with sculpted, muscular, shaved legs and perfect cycling kit—the form-fitting shorts, the jersey woven from expensive merino wool. Peeking over his shoulder, I saw what looked like a "1" on his license and assumed he was a Category 1 senior rider.

It turned out that Tony Comfort was fourteen—two years younger than I. (He was an "Intermediate"—a category for thirteen- and fourteen-year-olds—which explained the "I," which I had mistaken for a 1, on his license.) A cycling prodigy who unfortunately suffered an early burnout, Tony was already putting in three-hundred- to four-hundred-plus-mile weeks. He won that day's race, a twenty-five-mile time trial, outright. He was so deeply passionate about cycling, and cycling culture, that he eventually changed his name to Antonio Comforti. Later, Antonio told me that immigration officials on Ellis Island had changed his great-grandfather's name from Comforti to Comfort. Venerating the cycling culture in Europe—and in Italy in particular—he opted to revert back to the name of his ancestors. I respected that, and empathized. I was questing around for my own identity. We became friends. Despite our age difference, he became a kind of mentor to me, filling me in on the nuances and lore of bike racing. We logged thousands of training miles together. I remember that Tony's folks had split up, and that he lived with his mom and two brothers in a small bungalow near the CU campus. He spoke of his father, who lived in California, and whom he rarely saw, with reverence. One of the things cycling gave Tony was an outlet, an escape. That's what it gave me, too.

Not knowing what I was doing didn't prevent me from nailing down some decent results. By taking second in the 1976 Colorado state road race championships—some skinny guy named Ron Kiefel won it—I qualified for the nationals in Louisville, Kentucky. My father agreed to drive me out there for the race. Oh yeah—we were goin' to the nats! I was pumped! My euphoria would be short-lived.

I have vivid, selective memories of that road trip. A couple of days before the race, we parked next to a family from Reno who had brought along parents as well as grandparents. The bike racer in the family was a jug-eared fourteen-year-old with a ready grin and a background in freestyle skiing. I was sixteen and, like I said, starting to feel my oats. We were racing in different age groups, but that would not always be the case. Looking across at my future rival, I thought, *Dude, I'm gonna eat your lunch.*

In fact, I did not eat Greg LeMond's lunch that year, or any year in the foreseeable future.

By this time I'd borrowed some cool wheels that were supposed to be reserved just for races. But I trained on them when I wanted to feel fast, and I always wanted to feel fast. Just before the race started, I took a look at the tires and realized that they were *way* too worn for me to race on them. Uh-oh. Too embarrassed to say anything, I prayed to the cycling gods for benevolence. Two hundred meters into the seventy-mile race, I heard the air hissing out of my rear wheel. Took me *forever* to get it changed.

Dad had staked out a spot on a hill where he planned to hand me a water bottle. He dutifully cheered as the big pack flew past, not seeing me but certain I was tucked in there somewhere. Minutes later he spied a lone, wretched figure making his way up the climb. "Poor bastard," Damon recalled thinking. "I feel sorry for that kid's parents." Soon enough, he realized that *he* was one of that kid's parents. I compounded the humiliation by squirting some tears—right there, on the bike—when I saw him. It was our first big event together, we'd driven *so* far, and I'd screwed things up royally. I'd disappointed myself, and him. Afterward, I shared with him my tale of woe. He was sympathetic but unable to disguise his incredulity. He fixed me with a look that said, How stupid can you get?

We exchanged about a dozen sentences on the thousand-mile drive back to Boulder. The first thing Dad did when we got home was buy me new tires.

By 1977 I was starting to get the hang of it. In Milwaukee, I finished second to LeMond in total points at a prestigious series of races called SuperWeek. At the nationals in Seattle I took tenth in the time trial. As long as we were in the Northwest, Dad and I thought we'd drive up to Vancouver, where I entered my first race against an international field of senior riders, the Gastown Grand Prix. As I railed the corners and held my own with the older, more established guys, a spectator standing behind my father exclaimed, "Wow! Who is that young fellow? He's destined to do something in this sport!"

That overheard remark, followed by my result—I jumped into a breakaway and finished third—helped convince my old man that this fickle avocation might actually be my true calling. We'd come through some tense months. I'd just graduated from high

school, and I was either going to pursue racing as a full-time career or go to college. I'd been getting versions of the same lecture
for two-plus years: interesting and exotic as it was, healthful and
character building as it was, bike racing was a *hobby*, not a career. It was on this extended road trip that we reached some new
understanding, and the tension between us began to ebb. It's not
like Damon suddenly became a font of warmth and intimate conversation (although he would eventually, miraculously, get there).
But he was finally wrapping his head around the fact that my
post–high school education might end up being rather less formal than his.

It was on that trip that we met the Chews, an awesome cycling
family from the Squirrel Hill section of Pittsburgh, Pennsylvania. Tom Chew, a super-strong rider my age, invited me to join
his team in a couple of weeks at a big stage race in the province of
Quebec. I said I'd think about it and headed home with Dad. On
the fifteen-hundred-mile drive from Vancouver to Boulder, our
'73 microbus crapped out a couple of times. I remember sitting on
the side of the road outside Yakima, Washington, as Damon pulled
out the tools to fix the faulty alternator. He proceeded to stun me
by looking around from the engine compartment and saying, casually, "Why don't you go do that race in Canada?"

I did, and sprinted to victory in two stages of a premier junior
event called the Tour de l'Abitibi. (The race would be won thirty
years later by a young American named Taylor Phinney.) I spent
that autumn crashed at Chez Chew, going up against some surprisingly stiff competition in Thursday-night races around the
parking lot at the Pittsburgh Zoo. My season ended abruptly one
afternoon in the city's Highland Park, when Tom and I were goof-
ing around, jostling for position on our bikes. Just as I reached out
to grab him, he pulled away. Losing my balance, I hit the deck,
cracking my scapula in two. Recounting the incident a few days
later for my father, who picked me up at the Denver airport, I tried
to communicate to him the spirit of laughter and horseplay that

had led to the accident. Damon was not amused. Cracked scapula or not, he told me, I was going to have to find a job.

The big sky never gets old.

Returning to Colorado from, say, New England or Europe or the Midwest, I am invariably struck anew by the vastness of the sky over my home state. Even on a bad day, when my face is a mask and I feel like a hostage inside this twitching body, the sight of that endless blue dome — it frees me, somehow. There is something liberating, exhilarating, about the vast open spaces of the West, a grandness of scale that lured my father from back east and is a tonic for me to this day.

Here's the deal: when you're living in a Parkinson's body, your focus is, necessarily, internal. Am I shaking? How does my voice sound? How is my gait? How is my arm-swing when I walk?

We become so inward looking, so wrapped up in what's going on in our bodies, it becomes a kind of prison. But there is something about returning to Colorado, looking up at the big sky, that draws one out of self-immersion, invites the spirit to soar. In those moments, I transcend my malady.

The ability to escape my circumstances, if only in my mind, is one I've been honing since at least the early months of 1978, when I inherited a stack of magical magazines that transported me beyond the thin walls of a cramped Tucson apartment to exotic, faraway locales. And no, I'm not talking about the *SI* swimsuit issue.

One of the brightest lights in American cycling in the late '70s was a University of Arizona undergrad named Bob Cook, whose wire-rimmed spectacles gave him a professorial air and belied the fact that he would rip your legs off on a mountain ride. Rail thin and massively talented, Cook was one of the best climbers in the world, a kind of Human Lung who, during a visit to the Olympic Training Center in Colorado Springs, was found to have the highest oxygen intake (VO_2 max) of any cyclist ever tested to that time.

Fiercely competitive on the bike, he was no less generous with his time and counsel off of it.

So I was flattered and excited when Bob invited me to train with him in Tucson in the winter preceding the '78 season — almost as pumped as Damon was to get me out from under his roof. Even though I was training at least a couple of hours during the day, and busing tables at night, it rankled my father to see me haunting his house. The sight of his eighteen-year-old son sleeping in, keeping irregular hours, powering through alarming amounts of groceries — all of this offended his work ethic and Yankee frugality. So the relief was mutual when I said goodbye to my parents and headed for Arizona. Most of my friends were off to college. I didn't realize it as I headed for the desert, but I was about to enroll in a kind of school, myself.

In those days, outside Europe the sport of cycling was overlooked by sponsors and media alike. In the United States, cycling remained more cult than sport, a status that, if anything, increased its appeal to me. In the cold winter months of '78, the American epicenter of this cult sport, this esoteric, fringe avocation, became Tucson, where Cook and his friends and a cross section of riders from all over the country would train and talk about their shared passion. Those six weeks in the orbit of the man called the Cookie Monster constituted my first real taste of "the Life" — full immersion in this mysterious culture. And one of the cold truths about the Life was that the suffering wasn't limited to time in the saddle. Nobody had much money, and one was often forced to rely on the kindness of strangers. A friend of Bob's had an unoccupied room in his apartment and told me I was welcome to crash there, free of charge. Early every morning I'd head downtown to join Bob and his entourage of training partners for a ride. When it was over, Cook hustled over to the University of Arizona campus, where he was maintaining a 4.0 GPA. And I would pursue my own, less structured education.

Following a nap and a nourishing, inexpensive lunch (read:

PB&J), but before heading out on an easy afternoon recovery ride, I'd spend an hour or two in the Pyrenees, or Flanders, or Dunkirk, sometimes ranging as far afield as Cape Town or Corsica or Dublin — often accompanied by such legendary riders as the voracious Belgian Eddy Merckx, or France's hard-luck Raymond Poulidor, or the indefatigable Joop Zoetemelk of Holland. My ticket to these destinations was a gleaming stack of *International Cycle Sport* magazines, bequeathed to me by a fellow rider, Brian Smith, a cycling prodigy with a bottomless appetite for news of the sport he loved. A tremendous bargain at 40 pence per issue (I still remember the price stamped on each cover), *ICS* was the only English-language publication devoted to covering the European cycling scene. I devoured them, learning to look for bylines (John Wilcockson, Phil Liggett), coveting the jerseys and bike frames. I admired the style and panache of the Italians, the working-class grit of the Belgians. I memorized the results of events ranging from the Giro d'Italia to the British Milk Race. Had there been a written test, I'd have aced it.

There were about forty of them stacked in that apartment, and every edition was a portkey. Sitting in the middle of the desert, I was transported to the mud-slicked cobbles of Paris-Roubaix, could see the snowcapped Apennines crested by contestants of Milan–San Remo, could feel the crosswinds rending the peloton in Ghent-Wevelgem. They were all in those pages: the roads I wanted to ride, races I longed to contest. They felt so tangible and real, as I read those magazines, that when I did finally make it to the Show, when I started racing and getting results in Europe, it honestly felt as if I'd been there before.

Another signal event from those weeks in Tucson: I was formally introduced to a tall redhead who also happened to be the strongest female cyclist in America. Not yet twenty-one, Connie Carpenter was already in a league of her own. Not that she gave me *that* much face time. She was out of my league and, at nearly six feet, over my head. Plus, she was in Tucson with a guy named George Mount, who at that time was near the pinnacle of American cycling. Mount had finished sixth in the '76 Olympic road race — an incredible result for an American rider in those days. He was talented . . . and brash, and a little loud for my taste. I didn't have much to say to George, although I did wonder, *What does she see in him?* But Connie was kind enough to carry on a few conversations with me, and I left Arizona convinced that I'd made a good impression on her. What it boils down to, I'm fairly certain, is that chicks dig sprinters.

While they might be into sprinters, women are less attracted, in my experience, to *homeless* sprinters, which is why I was fortunate to know the generous Bob Firth, manager of the Three Rivers Bicycle Club in Pittsburgh. After securing McDonald's as a title sponsor for the '78 season, Bob offered to pay some of my race expenses and give me a place to stay. He let me flop in a tiny anteroom in his Squirrel Hill apartment. I maximized the space by removing the doors of the closet, which was just wide enough to accommodate an exceedingly narrow single mattress. A bachelor pad it wasn't.

Before the season started in Pennsylvania, Bob organized a two-week "training camp" at a boarded-up campsite deep in deer-hunting country. We stayed in a musty cabin. It rained hard, and often. Every other rider except one, a teammate named Maurice Holahan, bailed on the camp after a few days. I would've bailed too, but it would have hurt Bob's feelings. I had to live with the guy. Maurice and I had no car, and no way to get to a Laundromat, so our clothes never dried, we never got all the way warm or felt all the way fed. It was spartan and miserable and, as such, ideal preparation for what lay ahead on the other side of the Atlantic. I didn't complain. Much. This was the life I'd chosen. This was the Life.

I was learning how to train, how to race smarter, how to suffer. My results reflected that improvement. Entering events up and down the Eastern Seaboard, from Connecticut to North Carolina and many points in between, I found myself getting more consistent placings. Even if I didn't win, I could usually nail down a few primes (pronounced "preems," short for *premiums*) in the criteriums. Primes were usually cash prizes for sprints within a race, to keep the crowd interested. They also served the useful purpose of keeping guys like me from starving, or having to beg gas money to get home after a race. I took so many primes early in my career that race promoter Michael Aisner gave me the nickname the Cash Register.

I noticed, during this time, that I was spending more and more time on the phone with Damon, who waited for my calls on Sunday evening. If I didn't call, it meant I hadn't raced well that week. One night I phoned with especially good news: my team, Three Rivers, had been invited to ride in the biggest, best race in the country. Three years after my epiphany at North Boulder Park, I would now be on the other side of that fence, bumping bars with some of the best riders in the world at the Red Zinger Classic. I was coming full circle. I was coming home.

Estranged under the same roof for much of my adolescence, Dad and I had been retooling our relationship since I left the house. I burned to make him proud of me. During those Sunday-night phone calls, we started building a bridge to each other. It marked a significant step when Dad decided to take time off from his day job for the duration of the 1978 Red Zinger. He and Hal Chew—Tom's dad—were conscripted into service as official team drivers for the McDonald's/TRBC team. Damon's transition from aerospace engineer to team car driver and overall "fixer" went surprisingly smoothly. It made me happy, drawing him further and further into my world.

That year's field featured teams from Australia, Colombia, Mexico, Switzerland, Holland, Great Britain, and New Zealand. There was a US national team, plus Team Indy USA, featuring the brilliant Stetina brothers, Dale and Wayne. The Stetinas were a legendary cycling clan who ventured forth from their Indiana lair in

a hulking, ancient motor home known throughout the velo-uni-
verse as "the Ark." Piloted by the family patriarch, Roy Stetina,
a wiry, vociferous fixture on the national racing scene, the Ark
served as a kind of prototype for the vans and gleaming coaches
in which teams travel today. By its presence in the parking lot, the
Ark bestowed instant legitimacy on a given race. The Stetinas were
that good.

Traveling in more modest fashion was a constellation of smaller
squads like mine, Three Rivers, and the green-jerseyed members
of team Life Force Sprouts, led by my bespectacled friend and
mentor, Bob Cook. Bob startled the Colombian climbing specialists by attacking at the base of Battle Mountain on the third day of
the race, a ninety-eight-mile ordeal from Aspen to Vail that took
us over the Continental Divide — and 12,095-foot Independence
Pass. (That was 3,000 feet higher than the highest climb in the history of the Tour de France, and an untold number of feet higher
than the grandest eminences of my Pittsburgh training grounds.)

Only one rider, a Colombian named Plinio Casas, could stay
with Bob, and it was Casas who had more at the finish. Still, second was a great result for Bob. Chew and I straggled in with the
gruppetto — the band of survivors (often the sprinters) that comes
together well behind the leaders of every mountain stage. We were
shelled and parched and wondering how the hell we were going
to make it to the finish in Vail, let alone ride the next stage. All
the misery, the road rash and seared lungs, faded to insignificance
the following day. In a circuit race around Vail, I surprised everyone, myself included, by taking third. Third place, against a top
international field, for a guy who'd been racing only three years?
Are you kidding me? I didn't step up onto the podium that day — I
floated. I don't know that I'd ever seen my dad looking prouder.

That effort in Vail was one of those results that meant very little
to anyone but me. I would go on to win twenty-two stages of the
Coors Classic, which replaced the Red Zinger in 1980, not including the afternoon I sprinted for the "Rodeo Days" sign in down-

town Truckee, mistaking it for the finish line, thus handing a stage win to Bernard Hinault. (Not that that still gnaws at me or anything.) In 1988 I won the overall title outright. But that third-place finish a decade earlier did as much to propel me forward as any of the feats that followed.

I carried that confidence into SuperWeek, cleaning up against some of the country's best riders. I won the flashiest stage, a criterium in downtown Milwaukee in front of a great crowd, beating none other than the man himself, Wayne Frickin' Stetina, the defending national champion in the road race.

My profile was rising, but not so much that success ever threatened to go to my head. Cycling has a way of humbling its participants, as Tom and I were reminded each night during nationals week in Milwaukee. We stayed with my dad's twin brother, Warren, who along with his wife, Dorothy Ann, could not have been more welcoming. Alas, with three kids still at home, there was no room at the inn, meaning that we raced by day and crashed every night in a tent in their backyard.

I was now more than a blip on the radar to the Team USA coaches. Later that summer I was invited to a USA Cycling team training camp in Rutland, Vermont, where the US contingent boarded in the dormitories of a Catholic seminary called St. Joseph the Provider.

The pious influence of St. Joe the Pro, as we called him, did not prevent me from entertaining the occasionally impure thought about one Helen Conard "Connie" Carpenter, who was also at the camp. I'd occasionally find myself spinning alongside her on a training ride. Yes, she had a boyfriend and was light-years out of my league. But that didn't keep me from sidling up to attempt small talk. I didn't get the sense she minded so much. I found her incredibly easy to talk to. We laughed at the same things, but we weren't exactly headed in the same direction. She was on her way to the world championships in Germany. I wasn't sure where I was headed.

The following season I was invited to stay at the just-opened US Olympic Training Center in Colorado Springs. There, under the mentorship of a Polish defector named Eddie Borysewicz, Team USA's new cycling coach, I started getting the expert direction I'd been seeking for three years — sometimes more than I cared for. Eddie B. was determined to tear us down and rebuild us to his specifications. He had some brilliant ideas, and some strange ones, such as his belief that horsemeat could improve our performance. ("Guys, for me, horse is faster animal, so come on, eat horse." To wit, I always thought, *But what do horses eat?*) I never worked with a more *passionate* coach. And yes, we did eat horsemeat.

In those days, bike racing was divided into two separate worlds. There was pro racing in Europe, which is where we all dreamed of someday making a living; of zipping up our jerseys, then throwing our hands in the air after snatching victory in, say, Milan–San Remo or a stage of the Tour de France. And then there was the amateur circuit. That was the path chosen by most American riders, because there was no pro racing in the USA at the time, and it allowed us to maintain our amateur status for the Olympics. The definition of "amateur" varied from one side of the Iron Curtain to the other. Eastern bloc countries like the USSR, East Germany, Czechoslovakia, and Poland were cranking out "state-sponsored" amateurs who could've won nearly any race they entered, amateur or pro. Racing against those guys for Eddie B.'s US national team in the spring of '79, I got my ass kicked.

Our home away from home in Europe was a hotel and restaurant just outside the ancient walls of Bergamo, in northern Italy. The Bar Augusto was owned and operated by a family of deeply passionate cycling aficionados. (Italy is full of such knowledgeable, opinionated fans: they are called *tifosi*.) Inside the bar, cycling history was brought to life by scores of framed, colorful jerseys hanging from the walls. Everyone who is anyone in cycling, it seemed, had a signed jersey in the Bar Augusto, including a *maglia rosa* sported by the iconic Fausto Coppi—the pink leader's jersey gained during one of Coppi's Giro d'Italia victories.

The truth is, after a day in which I'd been gutted by smarter, stronger, and more seasoned European riders, those jerseys sometimes silently mocked me, calling attention to the vast gulf between my ambitions and my actual abilities. Above the restaurant was a warren of tiny rooms with ridiculously narrow bunks, where I would often drift off convinced that tomorrow would have to be better, because it couldn't be any worse.

We Americans shared these no-frills digs with other teams from other countries. We would descend from our rooms to the dining room feeling physically thrashed, only to be seated next to, for example, the Czech team that had won so many trophies they needed a special, dedicated table on which to stack their accumulated hardware. Meanwhile—and I'm not kidding—we had a single, sad little trophy that someone had won for finishing something like seventeenth. It was the equivalent of a "certificate of participation," or reward for having "traveled the farthest." In this setting, we were learning deep humility. But it also made us hungry. Those guys looked like us; they slept in the same beds and were eating the same food. What was different about them? How could we get better?

I got a welcome jolt of self-esteem at that summer's Red Zinger, winning the Vail stage I'd placed third in the previous year. At the finish, it came down to me and rising Australian star Phil Anderson, who two years later would ride into the yellow jersey at the Tour de France. But I was coming up in the world myself. It was dawning on me that if I could make it to the final kilometer with the leaders, then everyone else was in trouble in the race to the finish. I had a kind of God-given afterburner, a gear unavailable to most guys, including Phil, on that day.

I was still a relative newbie in the sport, but I already understood two things: (1) I had talent — enough to win races; and (2)
there were guys out there with a lot more natural talent than I had.

How would I make up the difference? I had a hunch that I could
gain an advantage on my rivals by developing a training program
in the off-season — a time when most riders took a break.

My main source of inspiration was not a cyclist, but the great
Thomas Magnusson, a Swedish Nordic skier and world champion
who refused to let a paucity of white stuff one season prevent him
from getting in his miles. With a shovel and a wheelbarrow, Magnusson scavenged enough slush and snow to create his own track,
one meter wide and a kilometer long. And he'd simply huff and
puff his way up and down that skinny little run, sixty times per
workout. I read that, and I realized there was no reason not to apply that kind of intense commitment to my own sport. So I devised
my own off-season regimen: three hours a day, seven days a week.
Minimum. Pushing through intervals in freezing conditions, I was
sustained by the thought of my rivals lounging at home.

It did not pay immediate dividends. Back in Europe in the
spring of '80, I suffered like a dog. Again. Got worked by the Euros. Again. We watched the Czechs, the Russians, amass another
armory of trophies. Again. And had to pretend to be pleased for
them while we, the Yanks, could've fit our trophies on a salad plate.
Finally I gutted out a fourth-place finish in a race near Nîmes,
France. That slender result sustained me and tided me over for the
rest of the trip. One of the (few) bright spots during that stretch
was the company of my wire-rimmed friend, Bob Cook, whose future seemed limitless.

At that time, Cook was climbing better than any American ever
had. But after being selected for the 1980 Olympic team, then having that dream denied him when President Carter decided to boy-
cott the Moscow games, Cook had a rash of bad crashes. He began
to experience severe headaches and balance problems.

CAT scans and exploratory surgery confirmed his worst fears:

he had several tumors in his brain, spawned by metastatic mela-noma. Barely three months after the diagnosis, we were at his fu-neral. As his friends and family memorialized and eulogized him, I acknowledged, gratefully and silently, that if I ended up hav-ing the career Bob had always assured me was within my reach, I would owe a piece of every victory to the man we knew as the Cookie Monster.

4

—— — ——

The Amateur

TO MEET ME early in the winter of 1981 was to conclude that my prospects were somewhat slender. I had four hundred dollars in my wallet and a seven-year-old Italian-made Masi bike that wouldn't survive the winter. I'd just had a knockdown-dragout fight with national coach Eddie B., which resulted in my temporarily quitting the national team. I'd gotten an offer from a new team sponsored by 7-Eleven . . . and turned it down. (They wanted me to sign a three-year deal with an agent I wanted no part of.) I talked my buddy Ron Kiefel into turning them down as well. Don't sweat it, I told Wookie (so nicknamed because he is one of the more hirsute dudes you will ever meet) — we've got an ace in the hole. Yoplait was sponsoring a team for the upcoming season, and they wanted both of us. We would race for the glory of the world's best-known prestirred yogurt product!

So it was not a good day when we found out that Yoplait had pulled the plug on the squad, leaving Ron and me without a team for the '81 season.

On the bright side, I was in love.

After taking second place in the aptly named Wisconsin Milk Race — we were, after all, in the Dairy State — I'd attended a party at the Madison home of Connie Carpenter. Connie hadn't been in the Milk Race. Coming off a disappointing and difficult 1979 season in which she suffered a serious concussion, she'd retired. After enrolling at UC-Berkeley, she'd been recruited to join the women's crew team. Within a year, and in true Connie style, she helped row the Bears to victory in the national championship.

Having "lost the thread" with cycling and now single, she'd come back to Madison to enjoy a peaceful summer on Lake Mendota. She was pleased to host a party for her old cycling tribe at her parents' lakefront home.

It was a bit of a wild night. Thumper was raucously played, copious amounts of malt beverages imbibed, and various party guests ended up in the lake, in the wee hours, in various states of undress. One Brit, I recall, slept outside on the stone front porch, and appeared at dawn looking much the worse for wear. (How 'bout those Wisconsin mosquitoes?) The sight of Charlie Carpenter roaming the premises the next morning, collecting beer bottles, prompted a mass exodus. Connie and I were already out to breakfast, enjoying the beginning of what I hoped might turn into a much longer conversation.

A few weeks later she sent me a postcard—remember postcards?—to let me know that she'd be driving through Boulder on her way to California. Did I want to get together?

Did I want to get together? If Connie Carpenter didn't realize she was out of my league, I wasn't going to wise her up. She was bright, beautiful, artistic, and one of the best athletes I'd ever met. At the age of fourteen, Connie had made the Olympic speed skating team, finishing seventh in the 1,500 meters at the 1972 Sapporo Winter Games. She was a medal favorite going into the '76 Olympics, but a chronic ankle injury forced her to abandon the sport shortly before those games. Following that crushing disappointment, and at the urging of Sheila Young, who'd transitioned from Olympic skater to world champion cyclist, Connie took a crack at bike racing. That ended up working out OK for her. She would go on to win thirteen national championships, on the road and track, plus four world championship medals.

I wrote her back, telling her to be sure to give me a call when she got to town. What followed was a kind of whirlwind, accelerated courtship. By the time Connie left Boulder, we were an item. While that dizzying interlude had been wonderful for my personal life, it hadn't done much for my form on the bike. At a circuit race in Colorado Springs—with my new girlfriend waiting at the finish—I was suffering deeply just to hold the wheel of Ron Kiefel, my friend and future teammate. At that point, Wookie and I were the best kind of rivals, pushing each other to the limit in local races. He would become my best teammate and lead-out guy, the rider into whose slipstream I would tuck until the final few hundred meters, when I'd sprint past. But that was all in the future. Now I whimpered to him, "Wook, ease up just a little and I won't sprint you."

Wookie did back off a smidge, allowing me to stay with him. Wouldn't you know, once the finish line came into view, I found myself feeling *much better.* And much to Ron's surprise and dismay, I found myself physically incapable of keeping my promise. With Connie watching, I couldn't help but throw down my best sprint. I won. Wookie was *pissed,* and I didn't blame him one bit. It was a shortsighted, lame move on my part, and I'm just lucky he didn't pummel me. I did give him my prize money—the least I could do. (He paid me back in full a couple of years later by snatching a win from me in Boulder.)

My relationship with Connie blossomed, with a clutch assist from some cut-rate, $65 round-trip airfares between Denver and San Francisco. I made the round-trip numerous times that fall, lugging my bike along, getting some training miles in, in the hills above Berkeley, savoring the California sunshine, local culture, and Connie's company.

The problem with those visits was that, all too quickly, it came time for me to leave. We were crazy for each other, but Connie wasn't keen on the idea of a prolonged, long-distance romance. Her letters began to take on a certain . . . *impatience.* The gist of her message: I needed to move closer to her, or we needed to move on from each other. And so, one February day in 1981, I packed my green VW Rabbit (aka the Shark) and headed west. I had friends in the Bay Area. I could find a job. I would train throughout the winter. I would resist the siren call of cross-country skiing. I would see Connie every day and every night. Life would be good.

Her life, of course, was incredibly full at the time. Having retired from cycling, she was finishing up her bachelor's degree in physical education (with an emphasis in exercise science).

"Where are you going to stay?" she asked me, quite reasonably, the day I showed up. After some hemming and hawing, I asked if I could crash with her for a few days while I hunted around for a job and an apartment.

No problem, she said. And that was that.

Connie lived in the basement of a large house with four roommates she did not know well. Our subterranean lair did have one advantage: it had a separate entrance, making it easier for me to maintain a low profile. I paid no rent. I worked odd jobs — mostly digging trenches or doing demolition at construction sites. I'd spend eight hours a day swinging a pickax, then go out on a two- or three-hour training ride, then do it all again the next day.

Ron and I were racing as gypsies, privateers — riders without a team. Hell, for a few days, there, I was a rider without a *bike.* While putting in some miles outside Walnut Creek, I came perilously close to receiving a self-administered aluminum-alloy enema. My seat dropped suddenly, accompanied by what sounded like the crumpling of a beer can. The seat tube supporting my saddle had sheared nearly in half. Determined to finish the ride, I responded exactly as you would have: by finding a hardware store, then using half a roll of duct tape to stabilize the tube. Hey, it got me home.

Early in 1981 the International Olympic Committee announced that, for the first time in Olympic history, the 1984 games in Los Angeles would feature a road race for women. Seizing on the buzz created by this news, an Austrian company called Puch (pronounced "Pook") was putting together a top women's team. They wanted Connie, who asked my advice. I was honest with her. I told her that, regardless of the countless races and the half-dozen national championships she'd won, she'd bailed on the sport *long* before reaching her full potential.

Whoa. *Wrong answer.* I thought she might slap me. We were in a serious relationship, yes, but when the subject of cycling arose, Connie was royalty, and I was some guy mucking stables outside the castle. My opinion struck her as impertinent. "Excuse me?" she replied, her eyes flashing with anger. I'm not sure what she'd expected me to say, but it wasn't that. She decided to interpret my remark not as an insult, but as a challenge, which is, I suppose, what I intended. "OK," she concluded after considering the matter. "I'll come back. I'll ride in the Olympics, win the gold medal, and retire the next day."

Even as I smiled and nodded and agreed with her — *Win gold and get out? How cool would that be?* — I left unspoken my reservation that life seldom works out so tidily. But it was awesome to have her back in the game. I would drive Connie and her teammates to races, serve as her mechanic, soigneur, and chief bottle-washer. And, oh yeah, my work done, I'd then proceed to race in the men's event. One weekend in Southern California, racing with no teammates, on Connie's backup bike, against the 7-Eleven juggernaut I'd turned down, I took seventh and fourth on consecutive days. For a gypsy rider whose day job until quite recently involved laboring under a hardhat, I was having a respectable start to the season. My ego had something to do with it. With Connie killing it in race after race, it was imperative that I, too, elevate my game, or be thought of as the loser boyfriend who couldn't keep up. After those two top-ten finishes in So-Cal, a marketing guy from Puch, Bruce Beck, approached me and said, "You're pretty good. Why don't you race for us?"

Puch agreed to pay me $4,500. Total. Better than nothing. We shook hands, and all of a sudden I was a one-man team, riding for Puch's sister company, Austro-Daimler. I had a ride.

When the '81 Coors Classic rolled around, I pulled together a rag-tag outfit of friends, strong riders like Doug "Bullet" Shapiro from back east, and others I'd trained with in Berkeley. We talked a local Boulder bike shop—Pedal Pushers—into cosponsoring us, which meant that we would have a mechanic and a support van. Going up against the likes of 7-Eleven, the French powerhouse Renault-Gitane, plus the US and Soviet national teams, my little band of mercenaries and I would need all the help we could get.

Yet there I stood on the fourth day of the race, on my now-familiar perch atop the podium in Vail Village. Winning was always a high, but it gave me an added rush to beat the mighty Soviets—who'd been known to sweep the top five places in some international competitions—while flying the colors of . . . Pedal Pushers/Austro-Daimler.

Connie, meanwhile, had returned to the sport more dominant than before she'd left it. She won the women's version of the Coors Classic. She won the US championship in the road race and time trial. A week later, at the track nationals, she won another national title in the points race. In late August, she came in third at the World Road Championships, in Prague. When I saw a picture of that photo finish—all three medalists had crossed the line within inches of one another—Connie's position leapt out at me.

She lost that race because she lacked one of the basic tools of the sprinter. She didn't properly "throw" her bike across the line. In bike racing, your placing is determined by the leading edge of your front tire. In a tight finish, it's critical to pitch your bike forward, much the same way a 100-meter runner "leans" at the tape. It's a learned technique and an important skill. So we had something to work on. While out together on training rides, every time we saw a city-limits sign, we'd sprint for it, and throw our bikes as we crossed the line. Connie quickly got the hang of it. It would pay big dividends later.

On a chilly, overcast day in May 2004, I endured more on a bicycle than I ever had during my pro career. Scrapping my way over the 9,045-foot Passo dello Stelvio, the highest mountain pass in Italy, was one of the hardest things I ever did.

Four years after my diagnosis, riding up the Stelvio with Connie and some of our Bike Camp clients, I wasn't getting much oomph from my left side. My poor right leg had to do 70 percent of the work. I quickly fell behind my clients, who were forced to wait for me at the summit while I basically willed my way, one-legged, up one of the most daunting climbs in Europe. The ascent goes on for thirty or so kilometers, but I must've logged an extra 10k that day by zigzagging up the grade, a humbling expedient known in cycling as "the paperboy."

I cursed, I prayed (though I am not especially religious), I may have shed a tear or two, but patience ruled the day. Keeping me upright and pedaling was the knowledge that, seven years earlier, with cancer ravaging his body, my father had made his methodic way up this beast. That trip to Europe, in fact, was Damon's last hurrah: the day after he summited the Stelvio, he boarded a flight back to the States while badly dehydrated, then suffered an embolism in his lung that nearly killed him. He survived, but that emergency triggered a downward spiral that ended with his death in 2001. Pushing my way up the Stelvio four years later, I kept repeating to myself: *If my dad could do this with prostate cancer at the age of sixty-nine, I can do it today.*

And I did. But a climb that would've taken me maybe an hour and a half, pre-PD, took me quite a bit longer. My reward for finally reaching the summit? Rather than ride on, and escape the cold, Connie and our intrepid campers steadfastly waited—some for well over an hour—to give me a rousing cheer and a cup of hot cocoa. Can you say "victory moment"?

I will say this in defense of moderately paced hikes and bike rides: you catch more of the scenery, the flowers and vineyards and waterfalls, when you're not trying to get everywhere at warp speed.

Patience does not come naturally to a sprinter, and it was definitely not a strong suit of mine early in my career. Going into the '82 season, 7-Eleven made me another offer, this one without the onerous strings attached. I was in. Upon joining that team, I had to become a bit less self-absorbed. I was forced, at times, to defer gratification. I learned—or started to learn—the importance of being patient. It was not a lesson that took root right away.

Riding with a group of stars, a bunch of guys at least as talented as I was, took some getting used to. Lacking a solid team around me up to that point, I was accustomed to attacking when the spirit moved me—riding for myself, basically. Now I had to reconcile my own ambitions with the need to be a team guy. Graciousness did not come so easily to me in the saddle. I was a nice person off the bike, but I could be a son of a bitch during a race. If our team had a rider in a breakaway, but I lacked confidence in his ability to win, I'd be antsy as hell back in the bunch, champing at the bit, spoiling to bridge up to the leaders. Because if *I* was in the breakaway, I was gonna win, hence the team (read: sponsor) would win—at least on the domestic front. Once in a great while I would cross that gap, unable to help myself, even though it is considered poor form to chase down a teammate. Yes, my rash attacks might lead to some harsh words in the team van after the race. On rare occasions, some of us might even find ourselves on the cusp of a fistfight. I recall Jeff Bradley screaming at me after I'd chased down a teammate during the Tour of Texas: "Phinney, you are so selfish!"

To which I replied, "Yeah, but did we win?"

I didn't care which of us won, I told my teammates, as long as *one* of us won. That was easy for me to say, of course, because I was the guy with the best sprint. Was I a solid team player? Or was I the selfish bastard Bradley pegged me for that afternoon in Houston? I started out as the latter but moved toward the former as I matured and gained wisdom and experience.

Jeff was right, of course: I was selfish. That wasn't exactly a news flash. Show me a selfless sprinter and I'll show you a sprinter who will be looking for a new team in the very near future.

My biggest rival on the domestic scene was a blond Canadian named Steve Bauer, a flat-footed pedaler and beast on the bike who showed up, I swear to God, in every breakaway I ever fought my way into. We were constantly slugging it out (figuratively) in sprint finishes. At the beginning of the '82 season — my first year with the 7-Eleven team — he continually got the best of me. There came a muggy afternoon in Cincinnati where I edged him at the line, and that served as a turning point for me. It gave me confidence that not only *could* I beat him in a sprint finish, I *should* beat him. Steve remained the better all-around rider. But if it came down to a sprint, I had the advantage.

The cycling world was bifurcated in the early '80s: the pros in their races, we amateurs in ours. (Like the strongest riders from the Eastern bloc, we were preserving our amateur status for the Olympics — a now-outdated concept.) On rare occasions, we would mix it up in the same race. One of those opportunities arose in June 1983, when much of the cycling world descended on Baltimore for the second running of the USPRO Championship. The 1.5-mile course, laid out along that city's Inner Harbor, was lined with eighty thousand spectators. By offering $50,000 in prize money — a more generous purse than any of the "spring classics" on the Continent — race organizers had lured a strong field of Euros, including Laurent Fignon, who would win the Tour de France the following month, and Irishman Stephen Roche, who would go on to win the '87 Tour de France *and* Giro d'Italia. As John Wilcockson recalled in *VeloNews*, "The North American amateurs were not given much hope of contending against the European pro teams."

But race day dawned muggy and hot on the shores of Chesapeake Bay. Bauer launched an attack, and formed a small breakaway with Aussie Allan Peiper, riding for the Peugeot team, and a veteran Belgian named Ferdi van den Haute, riding for Motobecane. Steeling myself for an uncomfortable interlude, I busted chops to bridge up to Bauer & Co. The four of us worked together and left the peloton far behind, then sprinted it out. Peiper led it out with Van den Haute just behind, but the Belgian didn't have much left in the tank. As he started fading, I hit full gas, passing him, then holding off Bauer over the final, furious closing meters to take the $25,000 first prize.

Watching the two pros fade was another, better-known Belgian. As Peiper wrote in his memoir, "Eddy Merckx was [in Baltimore] watching, and afterwards he came over to me and Van den Haute and asked us how we'd let these two amateurs beat us. He was very upset."

Not that I collected 25 large. As amateurs, we were allowed to keep *some* winnings — up to $200 per day — but not that much. And there was the matter of divvying up the cash — usually an even split among the guys on the team who were in the race.

USA Cycling held the leftover funds in an account for me, and cut me a check, with interest, after the Olympics, when I turned pro. Which is not to say I didn't reap some immediate dividends. I had just proven — to myself and eighty thousand people — that not only could I hang with some of the best riders in the world. On a good day, I could beat them.

What cash the federation could give me came in handy. I was in the market for a diamond.

In the spring of 1983 Connie and I were in Europe racing for the national team. One day she took the train from Paris to visit me in Blois, France, a hundred or so miles away, on the banks of the Loire. Connie was expecting some wining and dining — some *romance*, for God's sake! But I was zonked with fatigue, had no clean laundry, was flopping in a no-star, fleabag hotel, and had just crashed hard in a minor race called the Tour du Loir-et-Cher. Plus, it was raining. I wasn't very good company, apparently, which is why Connie cut short her visit. When she left for the train station, she was in tears.

I was left to reflect on what a heel I'd been. It was there, in Blois, that I told myself: *If I don't marry that woman, I'm an idiot.*

Five months later, in her parents' backyard on the shores of Lake Mendota, we tied the knot before family and friends. The vows we exchanged included the promise to stand by each other "in sickness and in health."

5

Ahab

IT ISN'T HEALTHY to want something as badly as I wanted to win the road race in the 1984 Olympics. That race consumed me as Ahab was consumed by the white whale. Like Ahab, I had some tricky crosscurrents to navigate. While my primary loyalty had to be to 7-Eleven, I also needed to spend time with the national team, showing up for training camps, racing in Europe, and most important, staying off Eddie B.'s shit list. He had proven himself to be a brilliant coach for some of the riders, but not especially flexible. In fact, he was completely inflexible, as one might expect from a guy raised on Eastern bloc authoritarianism. There was never much give-and-take with Eddie B. And once you got on his bad side, you stayed there.

Alexi Grewal got on his bad side. "I couldn't stand him and he couldn't stand me," said Alexi, many years later. A gifted, scrappy rider who floated up mountains, Alexi was fast and unpredictable. The son of Jasjit Grewal, who emigrated from India and opened a bike shop in Aspen, Alexi was drawn to cycling, he once told a reporter, because "it is nomadic, difficult and adventurous." That rebellious nature, the contrariness and impulsiveness that made him a truly *interesting* racer, also made him a poor match for our despotic, controlling master. Eddie B. would have loved nothing more than to exclude Alexi from the team for Los Angeles, but for one small problem: the guy won the Olympic trials.

While the rest of us were duking it out to earn our Olympic berths in the weeks before the games, Alexi was training on his own in Aspen. Ten days before the games, he tested positive for the banned stimulant ephedra during an in-competition test at the Coors Classic in Colorado, and was immediately disqualified from the event. Nothing if not forthcoming, Alexi copped to the violation in the press, explaining that he'd ingested the drug in a Chinese herbal supplement named Chi Power that had been given to him by his physical therapist. When Alexi's "B" sample came up positive, cycling's national governing body slapped him with a thirty-day suspension and dropped him from the Olympic team. At which point, Alexi took a different tack.

Grewal did have clearance for albuterol, to control asthma. Ephedra, also a bronchodilator, was in the same class of substances. Grewal's astute team director, Len Pettyjohn, enlisted the support of Dr. Richard Voy, chief MD for the US Olympic Committee. Voy successfully argued that the US Cycling Federation's testing procedure could not distinguish between the banned substance (ephedra) and the drug Alexi was allowed to take (albuterol). Grewal was reinstated one week before the games, getting off on a technicality. If not for this tactic, July 29, 1984, would have been a very different day indeed.

The men's road race consisted of a dozen laps of a ten-mile circuit around Mission Viejo, in Orange County. Race day was Sunday, July 29 — the day after the opening ceremony. Most of us who were contesting the road race took a pass on the opening ceremony and watched on TV from the comfort of our host housing, in and around Mission Viejo.

One member of our road squad, an alternate, did march into the Coliseum, where he met an attractive volunteer — an un-

dergraduate at USC, if I recall the story correctly. Upon learning that he was a member of the US cycling team, she asked his
name. "Umm, I'm Davis Phinney," he replied. As dawn broke the
following morning—after a rowdy night that included multiple
shots—she asked him, "Shouldn't you be getting ready for your
race?"

The women went first. They would ride five laps of the
course—just under fifty miles. The men did twelve laps. (Remember, this was the first-ever women's bike race in Olympic history.)
Because we'd married ten months earlier, Connie and I had been
marketed and hyped as America's first couple of cycling. Some athletes shrank from TV cameras and reporters. Not me. I wanted
that gold medal and wasn't afraid to say so. I remember sitting at
the kitchen table that morning, eating my breakfast bagel while the
sportscaster Al Michaels talked us up as double gold-medal favorites. Yes, I'd been living for this day, had trained for it and visualized it. I expected the pressure to be intense, and welcomed that
pressure. At least I thought I did. The more Michaels talked about
the potential for a historic double, the more I felt like a rugby
player being squeezed on all sides by the scrum.

After watching the start of the women's race on TV, I headed
over to the team reconnoiter spot. We piled into a van and drove
to the course. And it was only then that we got a taste of what we
were in for. Even in the morning, there were well over two hundred thousand people lining the roads. It was, by a degree of magnitude, the biggest crowd ever assembled in this country to watch
a bike race. I felt the pressure ratchet up a few more notches.

By nine thirty, it was 92 degrees. I sat in a van with a minia-
ture television, trying to make out the lithe form of my wife on
the tiny, black-and-white screen. Connie was a cofavorite in the
race along with the talented twenty-one-year-old Rebecca Twigg,
a rising star in the sport. The media had lapped up that story line,
the veteran versus the hungry up-and-comer. Rebecca had an irre-

sistible backstory: she was a teenage runaway who started college at the age of fourteen. Eddie B. filled the role of father figure and coach, which created a schism between Eddie and Connie. Her rivalry with Rebecca was intense and personal.

Those two were part of a six-woman group that broke away from the main field late in the race. Rebecca made a solo effort, but was chased down. The favorites were all in that elite group: the six of them would sprint it out for the medals. Setting up her sprint as they came into the long run-in to the line, Connie ventured a glance back, expecting an attack from the dangerous French rider Jeannie Longo. But with a few hundred meters to go, Longo was nowhere to be seen — she'd suffered a mechanical problem, it turned out, and literally disappeared.

In that instant, with Connie peering over her right shoulder, Rebecca launched her sprint up the left side of the road. Connie was immediately thirty feet behind. Back in the van, I was jumping out of my skin, shouting at the tiny TV, "WHAT ARE YOU DOING? GO! GO! GO!"

Swinging to her right, out of the slipstream of the Italian Maria Canins, Connie stood out of the saddle and started to wind it up. She had the length of a football field to make up ten yards, but she was hauling ass.

The Olympic course ended on a slightly upward pitch — a gradient *just* steep enough to break Rebecca's rhythm and take the edge off her sprint. In a frantic scramble immortalized in Bud Greenspan's documentary *16 Days of Glory,* Connie pulled even with her fading rival twenty feet from the line, then executed a perfect, textbook bike throw: back flat, head down, her long arms fully extended. She won by no more than three inches. It was enough. As the saying goes, the devil is in the details, and in that one race, on cycling's biggest stage, that one detail — the throw — made the difference.

Past the line, lungs heaving, the two teammates each draped an arm around the other in a rare embrace, their smiles incandescent. As they rounded the turn to where our team was clustered, Connie high-fived a few of the staff, jumped off her bike, and tackled me. While the crowd crammed against the fencing just above us went berserk, she shouted in my ear, "I think I won!" It was magic.

In January of 1985 we would learn, along with the rest of the world, that seven members of the US Olympic cycling team resorted to blood doping at the games. Rebecca was one of the seven — the only member of the road cycling team to undergo the procedure. Assisted by the national team coaches, those seven riders received blood transfusions to increase their red-blood-cell counts, in order to get more oxygen to their working muscles. The more oxygen available to the muscles, the higher the workload possible — an advantage in endurance athletics. The whistle-blowers were a disgruntled member of the track team and a US team doc. While considered unethical at the time, the practice was not yet prohibited by the IOC because it was not detectable. The method of delivery used by the US riders who went for it — receiving whole blood from a relative in a hotel room — was as ludicrous as it was potentially harmful.

Ten days before the games, on a trip to California to reconnoiter the road race course, Connie and I were approached on the plane by a team official who began rambling on about how one of the track riders had enjoyed great success at the trials by undergoing a blood transfusion prior to the race. The cyclist had withdrawn his own blood over the winter for the express purpose of reinfusion prior to the trials, hoping to improve his performance in order to make the Olympic team. The official went on to say that as it was now too close to the games for athletes to undergo this procedure using their own blood, the coaches — trying to gain any advantage — were recruiting relatives with blood types matching the athletes to donate blood for the transfusions. Incredulous, Connie, who had ultimate faith in her own *natural* ability, cut him off: "Get out of here. We don't want to hear one more word about it!" And that was the last we did hear of it, until the story broke.

Sometime after she won gold, Connie was debriefed by one of Greenspan's producers. Asked what the victory meant to her, she replied simply, "It was everything." (And ever true to herself and to her intention upon making her comeback, she in fact retired from competitive cycling the next day.)

If it was everything to her, the outcome of my race meant more, if possible, to me. And now it was time to sign in, take the line. Maybe my biggest problem that day was that, the broiling heat notwithstanding, I wasn't suffering. I'd trained with obsessive focus, but not overtrained, as I'd sometimes been inclined to do earlier in my career. I felt incredibly good. Too good.

At a brief prerace confab, Eddie repeated what he'd said at a "team meeting" the night before: that the basic strategy was to ride in support of the team leader — me. Alexi Grewal smiled and nodded and agreed and then went out and, in subtle, invisible ways that I've come to admire over the years, did his best to sap my strength, "stretch my legs," as he likes to say, and otherwise weaken me.

It was no small task. I was on the best day, physically, of my career, turning the pedals with such ease — almost as if the bike had no chain. I felt . . . invulnerable. The ten-mile loop featured two big hills — climbs I barely noticed for the first half of the race, during which I spent too much time on the front. In my hubris, I felt like Superman. Surely, if I didn't make any serious blunders, no one in the world was going to beat me, right?

That sense of invulnerability, of course, undid me. The Olympic road race is a different animal from the races we contest throughout the rest of the year. For one, there were extremely tight restrictions on getting food and water. In Mission Viejo, the feed zone was short and situated in a very fast part of the course. Normally, if you missed a feed or a bottle you could drop back to a team car to get the needed sustenance, but that wasn't allowed in the Olympic road race in those days. The result, for me, was a series of missed opportunities to eat. I felt so super for the first two-thirds of the race that it wasn't an issue. Rather, I didn't *think* it was an issue. But by relentlessly driving at the front of our early breakaway group, I was burning matches as if I had an unending supply.

One rider, it turned out, was paying close attention to my energy level. With around forty miles to race, I noted that Alexi's pockets were stuffed with food, and I asked him for something, anything, to eat. We'd known each other since high school. We were too competitive to be close friends, but still . . . Driving together to Wisconsin's SuperWeek seven years earlier, Alexi got pulled over well after midnight for speeding. We were somewhere in Nebraska. Next thing I knew, he was slapping me awake, telling me we needed to switch seats, yelling, "I don't have a license! I'm not old enough to drive!" Somehow we didn't get busted, and I felt like I'd saved his ass.

On that white-hot afternoon in California, my teammate heard my plea, stared straight ahead, and spoke one word:

"No."

Alexi recalled that drama for my friend Bob Babbitt in a radio interview a few years back. "Phinney had been asking me for food for two laps." The last time I asked, he recalled, "I was down to my last piece of food," which he described as a peach laced with the caffeinated pill NoDoz. "Had to deny him that. Those things make a difference." The caffeine I was unaware of, but the food, any food, I could've used. None was forthcoming.

Last year, out of the blue, he wrote me a very detailed letter, not exactly apologizing, but explaining his tactics and thinking on that day. While I'd forgotten my decision to wear a skin suit in that race, Alexi had not.

"It was the skin suit, Davis," he recalled. "I knew from the moment I saw you in it at the start that not having enough room for food would be a weakness I could and would exploit. And I did.

After denying you food I knew that it had to be that lap to break you." No mention of a spiked peach.

The decisive break had formed in the initial stages of the race: Alexi, two Norwegians, and a Colombian, along with fellow American Thurlow (aka Turbo) Rogers and me. What I'd also forgotten, until I received his letter, was that it was Alexi who'd initiated that breakaway. He attacked when he did because he'd seen Kiefel (whose loyalty to me was well known and unquestioned) "out of position." It was a clever tactic. With Wookie not in the move, Alexi had deprived me of, as he put it, my "right hand." It had come to this: the US team was racing against itself.

How was Alexi so well provisioned with food while I was running on fumes? It was my blunder, to keep missing out at the feed zone — and I wasn't the only one. Alexi, for his part, had cagily stationed an ally on an uphill part of the course away from the feed zone — a friend who adroitly slipped him snacks and bottles as we rode past, lap after lap. As Alexi himself has said since then, "Yeah, it was totally illegal, but that's life." If he'd been caught, he would've been disqualified. But he didn't get caught. Ten days after narrowly missing a DQ on a doping violation, he was still pushing the envelope in the race itself.

With a lap and a half to go, fifteen miles, a Norwegian, my future teammate Dag Otto Lauritzen, attacked. Everyone in the break went into the red to bring him back. At the top of the hill we reeled him in, and it was during that momentary lull that Alexi catapulted off the front, stunning us all. Thurlow and I looked at each other, both having the same thought: *WTF?! He's not supposed to do that.* The crowd was going ballistic. An American going solo in the closing stages of the race.

It was another shrewd move by Alexi, who admits in the letter, "I rode against you from the start that eventful day . . . It was a double-entendre sort of thing. Appearing to be doing all the 'right things' but all the while making moves and decisions that weak-ened you and Thurlow and left Ron out on his own in the field." If it seems calculating, it was.

It would have hurt to match Alexi's acceleration just then. But it was certainly doable. Working against me — and Thurlow — was the axiom that you don't chase down a teammate. Especially on national TV. Positioned directly in front of Thurlow and me, broadcasting our every move (or so we thought), was a motorcycle with a TV cameraman.

"What do you wanna do?" Thurlow yelled above the din.

"I guess we block," I replied. And just like that — we let him go — and Alexi gained a half minute on us with a lap remaining.

Later we learned that the motorcycle in front of us wasn't transmitting live pictures, and that the race wasn't even on television yet.

As it was, I drifted to the back of the chase group as we went through the final feed zone. I *had* to eat. Just as I was reaching for the musette, I looked up and saw Bauer tearing ass up the road after Grewal — whom he caught on the 12 percent grade of the Vista del Lago climb. I tossed the musette to the road and took off after them in a mad sprint.

A quarter century later, I recall nearly every pedal stroke of that final lap. I gradually closed on Bauer, but paid the price for my neglected sustenance, my hubris. Feeling myself grow light-headed, my legs got seriously *heavy*. Bauer was twenty yards away. If I could just catch him, I would hold his wheel, and he could tow me to Alexi, whom I would then spank in the final sprint. That, at least, is the revisionist outcome I've concocted in the intervening three decades.

In reality, like a commuter chasing a train in a bad dream, I never did close that gap. My legs seized up, and Bauer powered on to catch Alexi. Next, the Norwegians pulled alongside. They looked at me the way rubberneckers survey a car wreck, then pulled smoothly away. Alexi defied all odds by beating Steve in the sprint, winning the gold by a bike length. He actually made it look easy. Stunned, Bauer settled for the silver. Dag Otto Lauritzen took the bronze from his countryman, Morton Saether. I wobbled in a couple of minutes later in fifth place, just squeezing out Thurlow, who was sixth. Wookie made a late charge to take ninth. From the outside, it was a huge victory. Not only had an American rider taken the gold, but the entire team finished in the top ten. A historic day!

Just not the kind of history I had in mind. Fifth place in the Olympic Games. Not bad, right? I. Was. Crushed.

Seven days after the road race, I was one of four Americans who rode to a bronze medal in the team time trial. Honestly, while I rode to the limit, it was thanks to my teammates, Kiefel, Roy Knickman, and Andy Weaver, that we collected a medal. I'd shot my wad in the road race, both physically and emotionally. As the years went by, the significance of that medal has expanded in my mind. An Olympic medal — that's a pretty big deal, right? At the time, it offered little consolation. Looking back now, I have to laugh, thinking, *Dude, get over yourself!* But at the time, drowning in the vortex of self-absorption, self-importance, and ego, that was hard to do.

Connie and I had been a major story line for the American media going into the games. No married couple had ever won dual golds in one Olympics, let alone on the same day. With the world watching, she'd done her part, and in my view and others', I hadn't.

For months afterward, Connie — redheaded, statuesque — was recognized and stopped on the streets. Fans would say, "You're Connie Carpenter! That was so unbelievable! I was cheering for you! It was so close . . . you WON!" Then they would inevitably turn to me and ask in a somber tone, "You must be her husband . . . What happened?"

What happened? What happened, I came to appreciate, was that I'd chosen a sport that was both exhilarating and capricious. I chose a sport that alternately exalts you and leaves you on perpetual hold, listening to the Muzak version of "Gypsies, Tramps and Thieves."

The best lesson learned through my "swing and a miss" games experience? I found out what many have before me: that by obsessively and entirely focusing on *the goal* (the gold), I forgot to celebrate the process. While I would've found them irrelevant as an eager, impatient twenty-five-year-old, such concepts as "being present" and paying attention to the "now" are vital to me today, as I work to live well with a chronic disease. Losing the Olympics taught me that a singular, maniacal focus on any one goal is, in the end, unhealthy. The joy, it turns out, is in the journey.

6

The Big C

MY DAD HAD recently dedicated himself to riding his bicycle, but was nagged by pain in his upper right leg. Believing that he'd injured his hamstring, he consulted Andy Pruitt, never considering the possibility that the painful urination he'd been experiencing might, in some way, be connected. (How like my father — and his son, for that matter — to seek medical attention only when the discomfort got in the way of cycling.)

Scrutinizing an x-ray, Andy spotted a suspicious mass. In February of 1987 an oncologist confirmed for my father that, no, the pain was not emanating from a badly pulled hamstring. He was, rather, carrying around a grapefruit-sized tumor. Damon had prostate cancer, which had metastasized to his right ischium, or "sit bone," and into the base of his spine. He was fifty-nine. Doctors, using the staging method for prostate tumors, described his cancer as Gleason score 7, bordering on the most aggressive variety. His chances of surviving more than a few years were judged to be less than 30 percent.

Dad chose to hear in those words not a death sentence but a kind of cosmic wakeup call. In the months that followed, he emerged from his cocoon, his long emotional detachment. He began reaching out, engaging the world, saying hello to strangers on the street. At the age of twenty-eight, I became good friends with my father.

We discovered that we enjoyed each other's company. We started taking walks together. In 1981 Connie and I had moved back to Boulder, which remained my home base. Many mornings, I'd meet him at the top of Sixth Street, two blocks from my house. We would walk together through the field at Chautauqua Park, at the foot of the Flatirons. Or I would match him stride for stride on his brisk five-miler to work.

I got to *know* him during those walks. In his methodical way—with me prompting him, quizzing him, soaking up his replies—he revealed himself. His own father, it turned out, had been a cold and distant figure to him, which explained a few things. His family had known more than its share of tragedy and hardship. Damon regaled me with stories from his family tree, accounts of heroism, romance, and of the challenges of his own upbringing. In the evening of his life, my long-introverted father was suddenly outgoing.

Years later, long after the onset of my own chronic disease, I realized that I'd gone to school on Damon. My insistence on "living well, today"—the ethos put forward by my foundation—was subconsciously modeled on Damon's postdiagnosis determination to draw the full marrow from life, every day. My dad was already living strong with cancer before our mutual friend coined the word "Livestrong."

It was always odd to think of my dad as a twin: it seemed improbable that there could be two of him. But he and Warren were born on March 4, 1928, in Pittsfield, Massachusetts, the fourth and fifth children of Adelbert and Maria Theresa Phinney. By the time the twins arrived, my grandmother was forty-one—ancient for childbearing in those days. Adelbert was ten years *older* than she, and, by all accounts, already weary of the world.

In the sad interval between the birth of the twins and their next-eldest sibling, my grandmother had five miscarriages, which must have cast a pall over that house. The gulf between Damon and his older sibs was never truly bridged: he had little rapport with them for most of his life. Dad was a loner, which explained, in part, why he was drawn so powerfully by the open spaces of the West.

My father told me the story of his father's father, a sea captain who sailed out of Martha's Vineyard. Captain Phinney commanded a three-masted schooner named after my great-grandmother Clara, carrying cargo up and down the East Coast. One year, he and some investors bought on old sailing ship in Mobile, Alabama, refurbished it, then set sail for Cuba with a load of coal. That schooner was caught in a hurricane, with all hands abandoning ship except my great-grandfather, who, in storybook fashion, stayed onboard the sinking vessel and ended up, improbably, as the sole survivor.

The moral—at least the one my dad chose to latch on to, as he battled the Big C—was this: Never give up hope. No matter how slim the odds, never give up hope.

He told me about his maternal grandfather, George H. Dodge, who fought under Rear Admiral David ("Damn the torpedoes!") Farragut in the Battle of Mobile Bay. George had been born to wealth and privilege, but was cut off by his father for marrying below his station. He died when his daughter, my grandmother, Maria, was just one year old—leaving her mother destitute with five young children.

Maria's one great windfall came from a wealthy aunt, who shared her name, and paid for her to go to college. My grandmother's reverence for education was passed down to her children, and accounts for some of the trauma and disappointment Dad felt when I took a pass on college.

Dad was book smart and tough. After graduating from Pittsfield High fifth in his class, he and Warren both entered the Army at the age of seventeen, having qualified for a specialized engineering training program. After two years on active duty as a cryptographer, he studied mechanical engineering at the University of Massachusetts on the GI Bill, graduating summa cum laude. Despite his distance from his older brothers, he followed in their professional footsteps. In 1952 he moved to Lima, Ohio, to take his first job, with Westinghouse.

My father spent much of his time in Lima scheming for ways to get out of Lima — to western Pennsylvania and West Virginia, usually, for hiking or rock climbing. It was on one of these trips that he met Dorothy Ann Welsh — Thea, to her friends — who was down from Boston.

One summer he, Thea, and another couple drove to Wyoming for two weeks of backpacking and climbing. Losing his hold near the summit of 13,569-foot Mount Sacagawea in the Wind River Range, Dad tumbled a hundred feet down the rock face, coming to rest on a shallower pitch, the business end of his ice ax embedded deep in his thigh. The other couple went for help. As my mother, Thea, tells the story, she kept Damon warm by crawling into his sleeping bag. They were married by a justice of the peace, in Washington, DC (where Mom then worked), in 1956, after a long-distance courtship. They celebrated with a low-budget but adventurous European honeymoon. Again Mom picks up the thread, saying, "Well, your father wanted to get me a diamond ring, but I said I'd much prefer to go to Europe!"

It was Dad's great fortune, back in Ohio, to befriend one Tony Pranses, the Europhile son of a Frenchwoman who had married an American Army officer. Having spent his childhood in France, Tony had immersed himself in the lore of the great cyclists. He enjoyed recounting the feats of Fausto Coppi and Louison Bobet. Tony soon convinced Damon to invest in a bike. Dad bought a Raleigh three-speed and commenced training for, get this, a twelve-hour mass-start race in Pittsburgh. Their once-a-week training ride consisted of an all-day, 150-mile tour of northwest Ohio. They did the race twice, Dad's best finish being a fourth place. He covered 225 miles that day, despite a crash, on a forty-five-pound three-speed. Impressive!

After my parents married, they moved first to Denver and then to Boulder, where it was easier for them to indulge their passion for the outdoors in general and mountaineering in particular. Dad worked as a mechanical engineer, initially for Sundstrand, then with a company called Ball Brothers Research Corporation, which a few years earlier had made the move beyond manufacturing fruit jars to the aerospace sector. When Damon joined it, Ball Brothers had recently won a contract to build one of NASA's first spacecraft, the Orbiting Solar Observatory.

Damon Phinney's nickname at Ball, I later learned, was Damn Finicky. He came from a long line of Phinney engineers, and was a damned good one himself. His role at Ball gradually morphed into one of problem solver, a high-tech Mr. Fixit who was brought in to find flaws in the design process on various projects. Disciplined and meticulous, he became legendary for his unmerciful critiques.

Dad became well known in the cycling world, too. Annoyed by what he viewed as the exorbitant cost of replacing the "tubular" or "sew-up" tires (so called because the inner tube was sewn into the tire casing) then used by all racers — thirty bucks! — he taught himself how to repair them, a maddeningly involved process that entailed first finding the leak (not always obvious), detaching a part of the rim strip (a protective piece of fabric that was glued to the underside of the tire), then cutting open the stitching, pulling out the tube like so much intestine, patching the leak, feeding the inner tube back in without twisting or kinking it, stitching the tire *exactly* to original specifications so that it remained true and round, then regluing the rim strip.

He became so adept at this process that, ever the pragmatist, he started Western Sew-up Labs, which he ran out of our basement in true cottage-industry style. Long after I'd become a sponsored rider, with an endless supply of tubulars, he pressed on with his patchwork, fixing in the neighborhood, he reckoned, of four thou-

sand tires, at five to ten bucks a pop, depending. He referred to
that modest income as his "mad money," and used it to finance his
burgeoning passion for photography. The combination of the sol-
vents used for tire gluing and the chemicals in the darkroom made
our basement smell pretty toxic; in hindsight I've wondered what
role these substances might've played in his developing cancer.

Dad also taught himself (and me) the art of wheel building. He
applied a rocket scientist's precision and attention to detail to "lac-
ing" and "truing" (straightening) wheels — which he did to within
microns of perfection. Not having inherited the Phinney engineering gene, I struggled in my efforts to build wheels to his standards
(Damn Finicky!), which became a source of frustration for us
both. Later, he would teach his bike-racing daughter-in-law to lace
her own race wheels. With an almost Zen focus and ultra-calm approach, they would labor for hours over rim and spoke configura-
tions, producing perfect wheel-sets. Admittedly, I resented his patient tutelage and soft demeanor with her, it being so at odds with
the curtness I'd felt from him so often, growing up.

Dad had tried to be patient with me, he really had. But our
brains worked differently, which frustrated him. Where he would
look at a math problem and see the answer clearly, I'd sit there
mystified. "Why can't you get this?" he would finally ask, an edge
in his voice. "It's so *obvious!*" What I heard, of course, was, *How
could you be so stupid?* Before long, I stopped asking for his help.

Our slow-motion journey toward each other — from the near
alienation I felt as a teenager to the love and acceptance he later
gave me — was completed on those long walks, in the weeks and
months not long after he learned that he had cancer. It was a long
journey that had started, ironically, not long after I moved out
from under his roof.

His doctors described the cancer as "incurable but controllable."
It wasn't exactly a surprise to see him leaping headlong into his
new mission: researching everything he could find about his par-

ticular cancer. Dude was a rocket scientist, after all. And all the homework helped. But he got lucky, too. In Wisconsin, Connie's mother reached out to her circle of friends in the medical community. Back came the suggestion that Damon join a drug trial being conducted in Colorado for men with advanced prostate cancer. He was one of fifty patients invited to participate in the trial. Two years later, only one of them was still alive. The story of my great-grandfather was reinforced — never give up hope!

To slow the spread of his cancer, Dad needed to shut down his body's production of testosterone. That was accomplished with daily injections of a drug called Lupron — "chemical castration," as he put it.

The side effects of this "hormone deprivation" were not trivial. In addition to decreasing muscle tone and strength, it led to loss of libido and virility — even as it encouraged weight gain — and the loss of body hair. To offset this "puberty in reverse," as Dad called it, he started riding his bike. A lot. And not just on flat roads. At a time when conventional therapies called for limited or no strenuous activity, my father found that nothing kept him healthier or happier than hammering on the bike. He rode several thousand miles a year — many of those miles over some of the most daunting mountain passes in Colorado and Europe. One Christmas, we gave him a beautiful handmade Serotta bicycle — a far cry from the three-speed Raleigh warhorse he'd navigated around Ohio. The Serotta frame was made of titanium, which explained our reference to Damon's anticancer drug of choice: vitamin T.

Dad established an online support group called Cyclists Combating Cancer (which can be found today at RideToLive.org). In early 1999 he met a garrulous, muscular ex–US Air Force master sergeant named Chris Brewer, who'd been diagnosed with testicular cancer at roughly the same time as Lance Armstrong. Brewer developed a website for the CCC, and put it under the umbrella of the Lance Armstrong Foundation. Traffic on the site spiked rather dramatically the following summer — which may or may not have had something to do with Lance winning his first Tour de France.

The urgency of his situation had a dramatic effect on my dad's personality. Returning to Boulder after the '87 season, I came home to a changed man. My father's transformation altered not only the way we communicated, but also the way I viewed the world and my place in it.

It's not as if he went from tepid to lukewarm, or from reserved to occasionally outgoing. Like a man trying to make up for lost time, he took the express elevator to Full-On Extrovert. Striding through the CU campus on those walks to work, he doled out smiles and bright greetings to everyone he passed. This lifelong stoic had become, at the tail end of his sixth decade on earth, a font of bonhomie. What struck me was the surprisingly high number of people who smiled *back,* and that felt *good.*

The power of a smile!

To this day, I've embraced the smile as a potent life-giving, energy-renewal resource, the more incandescent and genuine the better. The act of smiling has become the first-choice "drug" in my mental medicine cabinet. One of the most common — and saddest — symptoms of Parkinson's is the expressionless "mask" that the disease imposes on your face. My mantra to anyone and everyone but *especially* the Parkinson community is to practice smiling as much as possible. Being in public with Damon, once he'd decided to let his light shine, was to be constantly reminded of the power of a smile.

The tenor of our conversations changed. It was as if the cancer cells invading his body broke down old barriers between us. He opened up and told me about *his life,* much of which I'd never known. I told him about *my life,* much of which he'd never known. He was softer, more vulnerable and accessible. Where firm handshakes had long been his preferred method of greeting, overnight he became an incorrigible hugger. He started hugging me *in pub-*

lic! Who are you, I wanted to ask, and what have you done with Damon Phinney? I loved it. Thrived on it. This was a side of him I'd never seen.

Damon climbed the Alpe d'Huez four times in his life. He loved that mountain on account of its fabled place in cycling annals, yes, but also because its switchbacks are numbered. The big climbs, especially the switchback climbs, delighted him; Passo Stelvio (forty-eight SBs) and Passo Pordoi (thirty-three), both in Italy, were favorites as well. He liked to quantify things, liked to see the number come down as he rose toward the goal.

That same, scientist's hankering for numbers, for statistics, compelled him to keep track of how many miles he logged and how many total feet in altitude he'd gained on the bike after his cancer diagnosis. The drugs he'd taken had shut down his production of testosterone — emasculated him, in a way. It measurably boosted his self-esteem, massaged his ego, to knock out a century at a good clip, or haul himself over a couple of monster mountain passes on one ride. Keeping track of every mile, every ride, every road, every climb ridden, postdiagnosis, might seem compulsive to some. But it was Dad's act of defiance — his way of thumbing his nose at the Big C.

By early 1994, seven years after his diagnosis (never give up hope!), his cycling logs showed twenty-five thousand miles. All those hours in the sun and mountain air, all that time sweating and pushing himself up "the road" was proving incredibly effective at staving off his cancer. Hell, just being *outside* was medicine for him. "Spiritual rejuvenation," he called it, a phrase unlikely to have crossed his lips, precancer. Dad set a goal for himself: he would "up the ante" — gunning for forty thousand miles, to be completed by the end of the tenth year following the discovery of his cancer. It meant jacking his annual mileage up to five thousand a year, from thirty-five hundred.

By early 1996, with just a year to go to hit the 40k mark — and nine years into his remission — Dad had a setback: cancer cells that had been dormant were active again in his prostate and sit bone. (Unlike some cancers, Damon's could not be totally eradicated.) On the short-term plus side, his oncologist prescribed hydrocortisone, a steroid hormone that actually made him much stronger on the bike. Boy, did he revel in that! In his sixty-ninth year, he set personal records for mileage (7,100) and vertical feet ascended (430,000). Keep in mind, this was before Garmin GPS devices were the norm. My dad had to calculate all his altitude gains using topo maps. It was impressive . . . and, OK, more than a little compulsive.

When he flew to France in August of '96 with Breaking Away Bicycle Tours (a performance-cycling tour outfit with which he was a repeat client), my father was just 360 miles shy of his goal. On the second-to-last day of that trip, Greg Hogan, the tour leader, put a pair of monster alps on the menu: his charges would summit the Col de la Croix de Fer, followed by the Alpe d'Huez. Damon's odometer would roll over to 40,000 on the back side of the Croix de Fer. *If* he could get over the damn thing. It was no sure bet.

The Croix de Fer rises fifty-four hundred feet — just over a mile, straight up — in the eighteen miles from Saint-Jean-de-Maurienne. The climb kicks you in the teeth from the get-go: its first three miles average a cruel, 10 percent, gradient. Damon, whose secret for getting over those big mountains was to always stay in the aerobic zone, was immediately anaerobic.

At the time, Larry Theobald and his wife, Heather Reid, worked for Breaking Away. (They've since started CycleItalia.) They are smart, interesting people whose company my parents truly enjoyed. It was mutual. Along with his two dozen other jobs, Larry drove the Breaking Away van that picked up stragglers. If a client fell too far behind and threatened to disrupt the schedule of the entire tour group, it was Larry's job to talk them into the van — "Which you hate to do," he recalled recently. "It's like getting your race number torn off during the Tour de France."

On the early slopes of the Croix de Fer, Larry pulled alongside Damon to ask how it was going, even though it was obvious: my sixty-eight-year-old father was struggling. "I think you're going to be seeing a lot of me today," he told Larry.

"We'll do this," Larry assured him. "Just take it easy, and one way or another, we'll get you up there!" With an encouraging slap on the shoulder, Larry sent him on his way. "And immediately," Dad recalled later, "I felt normal again!" Ah, the power of a word of encouragement and a pat on the back. Hope renewed!

He still had nine miles and nearly three thousand vertical feet to climb, but he had his groove back. Drinking in the panoramic view of the Aiguilles d'Arves (the Needles of Arves), a trio of soaring, serrated peaks across the valley, Dad finished much stronger than he'd started.

Standing before the iron cross that gives the col its name, he smiled as Larry snapped his picture, then he began the long descent. At some windswept moment soon thereafter — my father was never sure exactly where — he reached his goal and pedaled his forty thousandth mile. It was an amazing accomplishment that no one in the medical community would have thought possible upon his diagnosis nearly a decade earlier.

And so it was with elation, rather than agony, that he made his methodical way up the twenty-one switchbacks of the Alpe, ditching his bike at the top to join his fellow cyclo-tourists for sausages and beers. As was Greg Hogan's custom on days his group summited the Alpe d'Huez, he ignited some celebratory bottle rockets.

In the moments after she won her gold medal, Connie climbed into the TV booth with Al Michaels and Greg LeMond, in order to use ABC's phone. She was dying to talk to her parents, who'd stayed behind in Madison. The Carpenters' phone rang and rang, but no one picked up. Turned out they were all in the backyard, lighting off celebratory fireworks.

There was Damon, twelve years later, enjoying a modest pyro-technical celebration of his own. No, he hadn't won a gold medal. All he'd done was stiff-arm cancer, in the process carving out an extra decade of life—a life that he was living more fully, and con-sciously, than ever before. That was definitely worth a bottle rocket or two.

7

- - -

"We're Just the Americans, Man!"

MY JOB USED to be to ride away from people. Now I seek them out. Specifically, it has become my life's work to reach the members of what I call my tribe, people living with Parkinson's, living under a cloud, in the shadows, without hope. More than a million Americans have PD. A lot of them are suffering needlessly, having arrived at the conclusion that their lives, as they knew them, are over.

But there are so many things people living with PD can do to improve the quality of their lives *right away,* beyond taking the pills prescribed by their doctors: exercise, better nutrition, getting out and connecting with people — including fellow members of our tribe, who can be wonderful, insightful sources of support. Even though I'm now off meds, and leery of their often-profound side effects, I haven't always been, and agree there are times when pills can be a godsend. But I'm a big proponent of a positive attitude and the benefits of exercise — even if that exercise is only putting on a jacket and going around the block. Like the proverb says, "The journey of a thousand miles begins with a single step." All I ask of those who've despaired of getting better is that they take that step, and see where it leads them. I ask them to consider the case of Don H.

A few years ago I keynoted the Young-Onset Parkinson's Network Conference in Pennsylvania. Somewhere in the audience was Don, a heavyset, depressed, defeated guy in a downward spiral. Suffering some of the worst effects of both PD and its meds (including a compulsion to gamble), he'd alienated his family and put on fifty pounds. His marriage was coming apart.

I found all this out a year and a half later, when a smiling, vibrant, fit man introduced himself to me at a PD function in Colorado. It was Don. After hearing my message that night in Pennsylvania, he started pinpointing the positive moments in his day. He tied them together, "made a rope out of them," he told me, and used it to pull himself out of that dark place. His marriage was back on solid ground, he was riding his bike, he'd reclaimed his life. It gave me an almost inexpressible joy to have made a difference for him.

I remember walking through a hotel lobby in 2008, chatting up members of the tribe at my foundation's first-ever Victory Summit, a symposium for people living with Parkinson's disease. The vibe was terrific: people were upbeat, people were being nourished. Most people.

I couldn't help noticing Dan V., twitching miserably in a lobby chair, talking to Bill Bell, a DPF board member. A wiry man in his early sixties, he was there to attend the symposium but became so uncomfortable in the conference room that he walked out in the middle of a panel discussion. I wandered over and asked him how he was doing.

"Not so good," he told me. He wasn't on meds, wasn't getting good advice, wasn't getting inspiration. He was feeling invisible.

Bill asked him if he'd tried Sinemet. I mentioned the surgical option of deep brain stimulation. "Yeah, I could look at those," he said. "Or I could get a bullet and a gun."

Whoa! Wrong answer, buddy. "Look at you," I told him. "You're incredibly vital, you're intelligent, you have much more to give."

"Well," he said, "I used to think of myself as vital."

"*You still are!* You matter in the big scheme. You can't be cured—not yet—but you can be helped. And you *have* to find ways to help yourself. Because the option you just mentioned is *not* acceptable."

I gave him my card and told him I wanted to hear from him. Bill told me not long ago that Dan found a doctor who got him on the right meds, and that they've worked wonders. In fact, he said, the last time he'd spoken with Dan, Dan had just come in from a ride on his recumbent bike. In the snow.

The nature of Parkinson's is that the lights don't go out all at once. It's more of a gathering darkness that we must mindfully and methodically strive and push against. Life becomes a constant, conscious effort to get out from under a cloud. Sometimes we need a little shove.

A couple of months after the '84 Olympics, I found myself on an airplane next to a pleasant grandmother who'd seen Connie on television, winning her medal. "It was so exciting!" she declared, before adding this: "Her husband. I forget his name, but he was such a disappointment. I wonder what happened to him?"

I'll tell you what happened to that guy. He used that disappointment as fuel to launch himself into the prime of his career. The 1985 season marked the start of a great adventure for me and my 7-Eleven teammates. With the Olympics over, the time had come for us to leave the amateur ranks. We turned pro, and turned our gaze east. Until then, all of the great old European races—the grand tours and one-day classics and stage races in between—had always been contested by teams from that side of the pond. Pioneers like Greg LeMond and Jonathan Boyer had served as token Yanks on European squads. But no US-based team had ever raced competitively in the European pro peloton. The American Invasion, as it came to be known, was about to begin.

Thus did we arrive in the ancient cradle of art and civilization and manners—a bunch of guys riding under the banner of

that most American of inventions, the convenience store. Our
'85 squad — which included Eric "Gomer" Heiden, Ron "Wookie"
Kiefel, Chris "The Kid" Carmichael, Tom "Plowboy" Schuler, Jeff
"Brad-Dog" Bradley, Ron "Skin" Hayman, Matt "MEJ" Eaton, and
yours truly, Davis "Thor" Phinney — was greeted like so many bar-
barians at the gate. You could feel the chill, and I'm not talking
about the temperature. The vibe we got was basically, Who the hell
are you, and how did you get into our club?

We earned it, brother. As a team of first-year pros, we were
fighting for respect every day. I mean, some days it was a struggle just to *find* the race, let alone compete in it. Check that — it
was a struggle to find a gas station to fuel up the team cars so we
could start *looking* for the start. Then the race would begin — usually in freezing cold rain, that February and March on the Continent — and we would battle all day for position and respect, then
wearily head to the hotel, which might or might not have hot water, and wash our sodden clothes in the sink. Our jerseys never
quite dried, it seemed, and became grayer and more dingy as the
weeks went by.

For all that, we had some terrific performances. The Trofeo Lai-
gueglia is a mid-February one-day race that opens the Italian season. We took the start against such Italian champions as Francesco
Moser and Beppe Saronni, and a host of other notable European
riders. And Wookie smoked them all. Attacking the then reigning Italian national road champion Vittorio Algeri in the final kilometer, he won the race outright, becoming the first American to
do so. (The only other US rider to claim that prize has the initials
L.A.)

That night at the team hotel, a top Italian rider named Gianbat-
tista Baronchelli walked over to our table. Gibi, as he was called
(pronounced GB), had won dozens of races in Italy, including
multiple Giro stages, but was equally renowned for his extreme
discipline: he insisted that it helped his riding to remain celibate
for the duration of the cycling season.

Fortunately, he did not try to impose his asceticism on others. Flashing a warm smile, he called for the maitre d' to bring over some Prosecco (Italian-style champagne) and pour us all a measure of bubbly while proclaiming, "Complimenti ragazzi" — Congratulations, guys! That classy gesture added a grace note to our auspicious beginning.

Not all the Euros were as welcoming. I remember diving into a corner in the Trofeo, just jamming down on my right handlebar and railing the turn, like I did all the time in races back home. But if you didn't know me, and how I could handle my bike, it might have appeared risky and rash, which is why this creased veteran rode up alongside and in a thick dialect, laced into me. He didn't need to know English to catch the drift of my two-word reply.

The weather was so consistently miserable that one of my most valued possessions became a cutting-edge, stretch-fit Gore-Tex jacket — a first-generation miracle garment custom-made for Wookie and me by a Boulder company. In the final kilometers in the last stage of the weeklong Tirreno-Adriatico, with a field sprint looming, the time came for me to remove that jacket, in order to make myself as unencumbered and aerodynamic as possible. I hadn't planned for the eventuality that I'd need to take the thing off, unfortunately, and it was too bulky to be wadded up and stuffed into a pocket. *Hmm, what to do,* I pondered as the pace ratcheted up. If I tossed the jacket by the roadside, surely I'd never see it again. (The other sprinters, clad in cheap plastic capes, simply discarded them.) Have I mentioned that mine was a handmade prototype? And that we'd been having a soggy, bone-chilling late winter? The jacket stayed on. Guido Bontempi jumped hard at three hundred meters. I came off his wheel with two hundred meters to go, leading, leading . . . Damn! Nipped at the line by the Belgian Eric Vanderaerden.

But really, how bummed could I be? Second place for a neo-pro, in a prestigious race, was a decent result. So I was in good spirits back at the team hotel, until someone turned on the TV in the common room. There was a replay of the sprint finish, shot from a helicopter. You could see the sleek outline of Vanderaerden, in the blue and white of Panasonic. Bontempi was unmistakable in the bright red kit of Carrera. Between them: an ungainly, mud-streaked, bluish blob. Some of the guys on other teams started asking, "Who is that?"

"He didn't even take his jacket off for the sprint," exclaimed another. "What an imbecile! He could've won the stage!" They laughed. I squirmed.

"But you have to understand," I declared, finally feeling the need to defend myself, "it's a *really nice jacket.*"

Our next challenge came a few days later at Milan–San Remo, a race so storied and venerable that it's known as one of cycling's classic "Monuments." Being new guys on the block, we solicited advice on how to approach it. Our assistant director, Richard De-jonckheere, had a younger brother, Noel, who'd finished top ten in the race each of the past two years. Noel emphasized two points to us:

1. Eat and drink as much as possible. The race is long — nearly three hundred kilometers. Stay fueled. And . . .
2. Be one of the first ten riders at the base of the first climb, the Passo del Turchino, around 160 km in.

I was pleased — more pleased than I cared to let on — to arise on race day and see myself listed in the pages of *La Gazzetta dello Sport* as one of the minor favorites. My second-place finish in Tir-reno-Adriatico had not gone unnoticed. Bearing Noel's counsel in mind, I stuffed my pockets full with foil-wrapped panini (this was BPB — before PowerBars). I was carrying so much food that my rain cape barely fit over my jersey (crappy weather again, as usual, but still smarting from the criticism — Imbecile! — I chose a disposable jacket over the Gore-Tex — just in case).

We did a procession out of town, having rolled off from the

majestic Piazza del Duomo in Milan. Every ten kilometers or so, I would unwrap a sandwich and proceed to wolf it down until, around kilometer eighty, the Irish rider Sean Kelly, a *legitimate* prerace favorite, spun past. Taking note of my bulging cheeks — I looked like a chipmunk — and jersey pockets, he piped up in his high-pitched brogue, "What're ya doin'? Yer eatin' like a fookin' pig! You'll never make it to the finish eatin' like that!" Laughing to himself, he rode past, leaving me crestfallen. I'd just been mocked by one of my heroes! I immediately began tossing sandwiches overboard.

As we passed the 150-kilometer mark, the Passo del Turchino loomed. Mindful of Noel's instructions, I buried the needle to get up front. As did, unfortunately, most every other rider in the field. The ensuing bottleneck, coupled with our high speed and a slick, sharp turn, resulted in my being pushed off the pavement and into a ceremonial chain fence that bordered the course. I was largely uninjured — except for an excruciatingly painful dislocated finger. Thankfully, my teammate Eric Heiden stopped, sized up the situation — he was a future orthopedic surgeon, after all — and yanked the digit into place. I may have used a profanity or two during this procedure.

I tried to catch back up, but my finger — and morale — was shot. I'd started the day a favorite! And yet here I was, having been mocked by Kelly (ya fookin' pig!), way behind and chasing, where I should've been at the front. Pulling on the handlebars hurt like a mofo too. Eventually, I gave in.

As the team car drove past, our mechanic tossed me my rain bag, which contained extra clothes, and told me to wait for the follow bus, that ignominious conveyance known as the broom wagon. Too cold to stop, I kept riding, all the while wondering, *Where is that damn bus?* Misery preferring company, I was joined by a trio of other dropouts. Fifteen minutes passed. Thirty minutes. An hour. Where the f— was the bus? (Turned out it had filled up early in the race, due to the crap weather, and proceeded directly to San Remo.) Slowly it dawned on us that we were on our own.

Over the Turchino the course descended to the Mediterranean and headed up the coast. By now, the road had been reopened to traffic. We flagged down a policeman. He shrugged and kept going. We rode through the feed zone, finding it deserted. My hand was throbbing. I was acutely hungry. Why did I have to throw away *all* the panini? Plus, I was schlepping this unwieldy rain bag, the straps of which had long since cut off circulation in my arms.

Finally, in desperation, we had a group consult and split up, two guys continuing to ride to San Remo while a Belgian and I left the route entirely and rode our bikes up a short, steep climb to the entry point of the autostrada, where we startled the bejesus out of an elderly tollbooth operator. Pantomiming and using sign language, we explained the situation as best we could and asked his permission to hitchhike. As cars and trucks and farm vehicles rolled through the toll, we would stick our thumbs out and inquire, "San Remo?"

No one pulled over. Hell, barely anyone made eye contact. When the Southland Corporation, 7-Eleven's parent company, ponied up millions to sponsor a team, this was not the representation they had in mind. We looked like complete idiots. Adding insult to injury, as the afternoon waned we started to see, on the far side of the autostrada, team cars zipping past at two hundred kilometers an hour, heading *the other way,* in the direction of Milan. Uh-oh. *We're screwed,* I thought.

My new Belgian friend and I were almost in full panic mode when, as if in a dream, a 7-Eleven team car pulled up. Thank God! The tollbooth operator had phoned the police, who called ahead to their colleagues in San Remo, who'd found Richard Dejonckheere and apprised him of where we could be found. After dropping the Belgian off at his team hotel in Milan, it was 10 P.M. before we got back to our hotel.

Wookie, I learned, had enjoyed a much better day, and was actually in the top five going over the final climb, the Poggio. Eager to find out his official placing, he picked up a dozen copies of the next morning's *La Gazzetta,* only to discover that, due to a malfunction of the finish-line camera, race officials had been forced to take their best guess as to who was crossing the line, and in which order, as the pack sprinted in. Having misidentified Wookie, they'd simply seen the jersey and assigned me his finishing place. What can I say?

Sometimes when nothing is going your way, you just need to keep the faith, and have *hope* that things will work out.

Our learning curve that spring was as steep as the Poggio. At an earlier race called the Tour de Med, Ron was in a big group on a climb, bumping handlebars with a guy he would later describe as "this little squirt of a Frenchman." Riding alongside was Dag Otto Lauritzen, who hissed at Wookie, "Do you know who that is?" No, Wookie answered, he didn't. It was Bernard Hinault, the five-time Tour de France winner. There was Wookie, whom, several years earlier, I'd watched win the San Bruno Hill Climb, in record time, after taking the start with an epic New Year's hangover, banging handlebars with the legendary Badger, as he was called, one of the four or five best riders of all time.

That was a perfect metaphor for our experience that season: we didn't always know exactly what we were doing, or to whom we were doing it, but we certainly weren't scared. And we weren't inclined to back down.

Between Ron's victory, and Och's successfully hooking us up with an Italian cosponsor, Hoonved, a manufacturer of industrial washing machines (as if you have to be told!), we landed an invitation to the Giro d'Italia, one of cycling's three Grand Tours. It was a huge deal, a landmark moment for American cycling.

We were short a climber, so Och got in touch with the twenty-three-year-old Andy Hampsten. Admittedly, there aren't a lot of major ascents around Grand Forks, North Dakota, where Hampsten grew up. But we'd seen him drop the best climbers in North America as if he were flicking specks of lint off his jersey. Och signed him to a one-month contract.

OK, we had a mountain goat. What we lacked, Giro officials pointed out, was a team doctor. All the other squads had one. Massimo Testa, a bright young MD who had specialized in sports medicine at the University of Pavia, Italy, volunteered to fill in. He was studying to become a family practice doc in his hometown of Como, but as a former national-class soccer player, he had the mind of a coach and trainer as well. His English was great, his demeanor perfect.

Just a few days before the Giro, one of our linchpin veterans, Ron Hayman, got sick. Team director Mike Neel suggested Bob Roll as replacement, and with no notice Bob hopped on a plane from the States. On the day before the prologue, we took a little training ride in the country outside Verona. We stopped at a café, and felt more than a little out of place. You could see these old Italian men, guys who knew the sport, lived the sport, staring at us, eyeballing our strange jerseys, trying to figure out who we were. Suddenly, Bob started talking to them in Italian. We were slack-jawed. He just looked at us and said, by way of explanation, "Mike Neel told me to learn the language."

One of the old men asked, "Which of you is the captain?" And Bob flashed his gap-toothed grin and replied, "Siamo tutti capitani" — We're all captains. *I love this guy!* I thought to myself.

I wasn't alone. Despite his lack of experience in the pro peloton, Bob quickly became Mr. Congeniality in the bunch. He'd ride up alongside anyone, even Moser — the defending Giro champion, Il Capo, the Boss himself! — and just start shooting the breeze. "Ciao, Frank! How's it going? Are these some beautiful vineyards or what?" Moser loved him.

Bob had a gift for languages and he adroitly picked up smatterings of Dutch, Russian, Spanish, you name it. One day he rode his bike to the start line ahead of us, and when we got there he was holding court, regaling the media with stories of his "Wild West" upbringing, where he lived in a tepee! I'm not sure if the Bay Area suburb of Pleasanton, California, could be considered the Wild West, and I can't verify that he spent time in a tepee—but it made a great story, and matched the outlandish snakeskin print on his Lycra tights.

Even as they liked most of us individually, the Euros were inclined to look down their noses at the American riders in general (with the exception of LeMond, for whom they had tremendous respect). Every time there was a crash, they reflexively blamed us. To them, we were cowboys. We could be a mile behind the pileup and it would still be our fault.

Solidifying our reputation as outsiders, we introduced a female soigneur into the all-male bastion that was then pro cycling. Shelley Versus was, like Bob, unique and irrepressible. *La Bionda,* as she was called—the Blonde—Shelley turned heads everywhere we went, with her easy smile and big laugh. Initially, as with most things we introduced to the peloton, the Europeans were skeptical. But Shelley worked hard, earned respect, and blazed a trail for numerous women to follow.

We started the Giro with a sprint finish where I came close to winning, finishing fourth. Andy Hampsten, who was essentially right off the boat, was impressed. It was as if a light bulb went off in his head, then and there, as he stated emphatically, "We can beat these guys!"

Two weeks into the Giro, however, we'd won no stages. I had multiple top-ten finishes, but suffered light frostbite in my big toes when we went over the Dolomites, after which every pedal stroke was painful; every bump in the road, agony. Finally, on the rest day, almost crazed with pain, I whittled through my toenails with Wookie's Swiss Army knife, allowing the fluid to escape, which did the trick, providing instant relief.

Stage 15 was a long slog up the spine of the Umbrian region, from L'Aquila to Perugia. In the team meeting that morning, Mike Neel was down in the dumps. An ex-racer from California who'd been one of the earliest Americans to ride in the European pro peloton, Mike was fluent in Italian; he knew the terrain. He was an excellent director, though not above manipulating us, playing one rider off another to get the best possible result.

"You've GOT to get someone in the break today," he told us — *pleaded* with us — the morning of Stage 15. We all nodded and agreed but secretly knew it was an impossible request.

Sure enough, a breakaway group got away with no 7-Eleven riders in it. Not long after, Mike pulled up in the team car, sounding aggrieved as he ordered, "You guys gotta start chasing." And we all nodded and agreed. Then the team car drifted back, and nobody started chasing. As Wookie put it, "We're just the Americans, man!" How were we supposed to chase down a breakaway, in other words? We were just surviving out there, trying to get through the day.

We were saved by Moser's team, which got on the front and jacked up the pace to sixty, sixty-five, seventy kilometers per hour. We let those guys pull like an express train until we were within thirty seconds of the breakaway, then we went to the front, as if to say, We'd have been here sooner, but we got stuck in traffic. During the catch, Wookie's job had been to keep Hampsten out of the wind. We hoped to spring Andy on the three-mile, stair-step ascent to the finish in Perugia.

Having delivered Hampsten to the base of the climb, Wookie assumed that he could wish Andy luck, punch the clock, and cruise in with the main bunch, on autopilot.

"My thinking was, 'OK, I did my work,'" he recounted afterward. "I kind of relaxed and sat up, but then we hit this hairpin turn, which caused a bottleneck."

Taking an open line to the outside, Ron skirted the traffic jam and hit the front of the race just as three riders attacked. "So I went with 'em," he remembers. After reeling those three in, Wookie figured, "What the hell, I'll take a shot," and attacked himself, not knowing who was still ahead. With less than a mile to race, he overtook the former world champion Gerrie Knetemann, and thought to himself, "Who the hell else is up here?"

After pulling through hard, Wook swung over, signaling to the Dutchman that it was his turn to lead again. "He didn't want to pull," recalled Ron, "so I thought, I guess I'll just keep going." Turning himself inside out, he left the Dutchman behind as they bounced over the paving-stone finishing stretch. Even as he crossed the line, Ron had no idea that he'd won until a constellation of flashbulbs exploded. The look on his face — a blend of joy and surprise — was classic Wookie.

It had taken eighty-three years for an American to win a stage in one of bike racing's three Grand Tours. It took five days for it to happen a second time, when Andy Hampsten timed his move perfectly to seize Stage 20 in the Aosta Valley. We capped off our Grand Tour experience in style as Eric Heiden collected the overall title and jersey for interrace sprints.

Clearly, our team had arrived.

8

I Can't Believe It. I Won?

WHEN MY TREMOR was firing, or when the meds were wearing off and my upper body started looping like a Tilt-a-Whirl, I was *not* the guy you wanted to see coming down the airplane aisle, eyeballing the seat next to you. Trust me, it was a miserable experience for both of us.

I'd gone through life with the confidence of an elite athlete. Parkinson's took that from me. But there comes a point when you realize that self-consciousness isn't helping. It's actually quite liberating when you give in and say, "This is what it is." You announce to the world, "That's right, I've got a disability. Check it out, check me out, and let's move on."

What I do, once I'm settled on the plane, is look my row-mate in the eye, explain that I have Parkinson's, and tell him that I might do some tremoring over the course of the journey and that I hope it won't bother him. That invariably leads to a conversation about the disease, giving me an opportunity to raise PD awareness — and, often, to make the acquaintance of a kind or interesting person with whom I otherwise might not have spoken. I've rarely regretted my decision to break the ice.

I wish it had been that easy at my first Tour. Trying to get to the front of the bunch in the nervous, early stages of the Tour de

France was like trying to get a beer on a Friday night in a packed pub in a foreign country where the regulars are lined up five-deep at the bar. When you politely tap them on the shoulder, they ignore you. Tap a second time and you get a look that says, "Touch me again and we're stepping outside." They don't know you. They just know they don't like you.

Based on our European successes in 1985, we went into the '86 Tour de France with the attitude that we had nothing to apologize for—that we belonged. That, at least, was the vibe we tried hard to project to the world. We also knew that, as challenging as the Giro had been, the Tour de France would be a degree of magnitude harder. We'd heard that, unlike the Giro, there were no easy stages, no *capo* dictating the pace. And at more than forty-one hundred kilometers (twenty-five hundred miles), this was the longest Tour in a decade.

We were nervous, anxious. At least I was. At that first Tour, my overwhelming sense was of a nagging self-consciousness, as if a giant eye hovered above us at all times, an all-seeing entity that forced me to constantly ask myself: *Do we fit in? Do we look the part? Will we be ridiculed?*

All of those fears came to fruition when, on the very first stage, our teammate Alex Stieda surprised us by arriving at the start line in a one-piece Lycra skin suit. *WTF?* My amateur Olympic road race aside, no self-respecting pro would ever consider donning anything but jersey and shorts for a mass-start race. We, Alex's teammates, were collectively mortified. We were trying so hard to look the part, and Alex—having consulted none of us—shows up in this . . . unitard. "Thanks, Alex," I muttered under my breath.

A free spirit fond of breaking out his harmonica in the team car, Alex was a neo-pro from Canada, completely unknown to the European peloton. Just before we reached the halfway point between the Paris suburb of Nanterre and the finish in Sceaux, eighty-five kilometers to the north, he launched his covert attack. Making use of the universal "Peepee" — indicating he had to take a leak — he rode ahead of the bunch.

"They didn't really understand why I had the skin suit on," he recently explained, "just that it'd be troublesome to take a leak." As soon as he got around a corner and out of the peloton's sight, "I put it in the 53-12" — his biggest gear — "and went for it." There were no race radios in those days, no in-the-car TVs with live broadcast. By the time the guy on the motorcycle with the little chalkboard showed us the split, Alex was three minutes ahead. Because there was a team time trial in the afternoon, our competition was reluctant to use up precious energy chasing an unknown rider from an American team. As we grasped what Alex was up to, we started to smile.

Forty-five or so minutes later a small chase group of five riders formed, reeling him in with twenty kilometers still to race. In a display of sheer guts, Alex found the juice to latch on to the chase group as it hurtled past. That breakaway finished a mere two seconds up on the fast-charging field.

Alex ended up fifth on the day, finishing less than a second behind the stage winner. During his time on the front, it turned out, he'd been a busy little bee. He'd collected the King of the Mountains jersey, the *maillot blanc,* given to the best young rider, the red interstage sprint jersey, and the Maillot la Presence, for general excellence (both of the latter two *maillots* have since been discontinued). Alex had ridden a strong prologue the day before, finishing twenty-first. Now, thanks to a handful of time bonuses, he also found himself pulling on the race leader's fabled yellow jersey. By the end of awards ceremonies, Stieda needed another suitcase for all his new *maillots.* His cheeks were smudged with lipstick from trading busses with podium girls. He practically floated from the stage to the press conference — which went on interminably, and cut into his recovery for that afternoon's team time trial, where a different fate awaited. One of the most auspicious beginnings ever enjoyed by a new team at the Tour de France was about to take an ignominious turn.

I blame myself for setting the tone for our slapstick performance in that afternoon's team time trial. In that discipline, teams race against the clock, riding en bloc, or flat out in a pace line, trading turns at the front, then drafting off the rider in front of them. The rider leading is said to be "taking a pull." The sight of a tightly spaced pace line flying up the road "full gas" is among the most spectacular in sports. And then there was the 1986 7-Eleven squad, whose TTT might as well have been accompanied by the theme music from *The Benny Hill Show*. Again, I blame myself. We started off well enough, although everyone was slightly overamped by having the yellow jersey in our midst. Toward the end of a gradual downhill pull, where I jacked the speed up to near seventy kilometers per hour, I stayed on the front as the course veered left around a seemingly benign corner. I railed the turn, but realized too late that I was leading us toward a concrete median bisecting the road. Arcing my wheels deeply to the left, I missed the median. But my tight line caused the guys behind me to fan farther out to the right until Eric Heiden, with nowhere to go, nailed the median and went down—as did several riders behind him. We hadn't gone ten kilometers and already had a catastrophe. It only got worse from there.

After regrouping we were forced to play catch-up. Pressing harder than ever, we were on the verge of coming unglued. We argued. At one point Doug Shapiro launched his water bottle over our heads out of frustration. Ron Kiefel gave me the "We're in trouble" look—and indeed we were.

Alex Stieda, meanwhile, was in even deeper trouble. Exhausted from his exertions that morning, he bonked badly and was unable to hang on to the wheel of the teammate in front of him. We would drop him, slow to let him latch back on, then drop him again. A decision had to be made. We could wait for Alex—and risk having the entire team miss the time limit and be tossed from the race. Or we could cut him loose and wish him luck. Mike Neel split the difference, instructing Chris Carmichael and Jeff Pierce to drop back and pace Alex to the finish. Alex made the time cut by thirty seconds, then nearly collapsed after dismounting his bike.

Only twenty-one more stages to go!

The afternoon had been an unmitigated disaster. We plunged from the top of the standings to the bottom. Sam Abt of the *New York Times* asked me straight up: "Have you ever ridden a team time trial before?"

I got a little pissy with him — "I did win a medal in the Olympics in this event," I huffed — but his point was valid. We hadn't driven the course beforehand, hadn't practiced riding all nine guys in formation, at racing speed. That just wasn't standard operating procedure in those days. As a result of that debacle, Och vowed that no team of his would ever again be unprepared for a TTT. Nor has it.

It felt strange to be sipping champagne at that night's team dinner. After Alex's spectacular success that morning, we'd been embarrassed in the afternoon. There were plenty of people who'd taken pleasure in our comeuppance, who felt that we'd been put in our place. Nobody talked about winning the next day's stage, a long, flat, 214-kilometer haul from the outskirts of Paris to Liévin, near the Belgian border. Our goal was not victory. Alex went from yellow to polka dots, as he was still leading the mountains competition. We wanted to defend that, but mostly we just wanted to stay on our bikes and finish. We needed to recover, psychologically and physically.

There is every other bike race in the world, and then there is the Tour. The pace is faster, the competition fiercer to ride at the front. The temperament in the peloton is anxious, edgy, ruthless — almost unbearably so. The stakes are higher; behavior and tactics, more cutthroat. Crashes are more frequent, particularly in these early, flat stages. And in the '86 Grand Boucle, those crashes were frequently blamed on us. The accusations were often false. But not always. In one incident, caught famously on video, a 7-Eleven rider is seen glancing at a TV motorbike, which had pulled up alongside him. Distracted, he looks again, then promptly rides right into future Tour winner Pedro Delgado, who broke his collarbone in the ensuing crash.

I'd never been in a race that taxed the mind no less than the body, but that's what the Tour did. And does. If I didn't focus intently on holding my line, marking my territory and riding in front, I quickly found myself flushed to the back of the bus. It feels like you are swimming upstream, constantly. The art of it is to hold your position by continuously moving forward. If you are not moving forward, you are quickly shunted to the back — a place where I found myself quite frequently that Tour. And once there, I would invariably be in the company of a half-dozen teammates on their red Murray bicycles.

We rode out of Paris in a misty rain and into a stiff headwind. The peloton was about two-thirds through the 214-kilometer stage, somewhere in the Somme region, when these two things happened: the narrow, two-lane road opened to a broad boulevard, and at the same moment I was passed by a strong Swiss rider named Robert Dill-Bundi (the 1980 Olympic pursuit champion). Having dropped back to his team car, he was now working his way back up to business class. Taking the free ride, I jumped on his wheel and let him pull me up the side of the dense pack. Just as we reached the front, the boulevard once again narrowed. Seizing the moment, Dill-Bundi attacked, and I went with him. Ten more guys latched on, and within ten kilometers, we'd built up a two-minute lead over the main bunch. Just like that I was in my first TDF breakaway. Sweet!

I was excited, but tried to keep a level head. My pulls at the front were hard, but not too hard. You want the break to stay away, but you also need to hold some strength in reserve for the final sprint, should it come to that.

Before long Och pulled alongside in one of our follow cars — at the time it was the only way a director could communicate with riders. His first words to me through the open car window: "You know, this could work!"

"I know!" I excitedly mouthed back, all the while trying to exude a cool insouciance.

My fellow escapees included Dag Otto Lauritzen, the Dutch rider Henk Boeve, and Charly Mottet, a threat for the overall. Surveying the group on the fly, I saw some riders more experienced than I and some who were better climbers. But I didn't see anyone who could beat me in a sprint.

Behind us, the beast had awakened. Greg LeMond's La Vie Claire squad had come to the front and begun turning the screws. With twenty-five kilometers, we were still up by ninety seconds, but losing time in big chunks. Then we caught a break. One of La Vie Claire's big dogs — LeMond or Bernard Hinault — flatted. The chase stalled.

I was doing my best to stay in the moment — without anticipating anything too far ahead (like a STAGE WIN!). Yet with each kilometer that clicked by, I grew more confident and hopeful.

Then, just like that, my big chance went up the road. Federico Echave, a Spaniard, attacked. To my disappointment, no one chased. With the finish line less then twenty-five kilometers away, we were now racing to be first loser. (At a Tour stage finish there are no second or third rungs on the podium.)

At the ten-kilometer banner we were still forty-nine seconds up, but hemorrhaging time — five to ten seconds per kilometer. Once inside the city limits, the *parcours* was twisting and technical, which worked in our favor as it kept us out of their direct line of sight. (Nothing quite whets the appetite of the chase group like actual visual contact with its quarry.) The final five hundred meters took us up a long, slightly uphill straightaway. We approached the finish line at full gas, nine of us lined out, one behind the other. I was content to sit on the back, surveying the scene with a cool detachment I would not have felt had Echave not escaped—that is, had we been racing for first rather than second. From the roar of the crowd, you couldn't tell that the stage had already been won. At 250 meters I launched, digging so deeply that with just a football field to go I led by three bike lengths.

Playing it rather too casually—again, the race was now for second—I eased up twenty yards from the line, but felt a rider fast approaching from my right. With a final spasm of effort, I sped up and "threw" my bike, beating Henk Boeve by no more than three inches.

I was surprised to find myself immediately surrounded by a dense scrum of reporters, including John Wilcockson of *VeloNews*, who shouted at me, "Davis, that was incredible!"

Secretly pleased though I was with my second-place finish, I thought John was overreacting.

"Yeah, I won the sprint. But I still came in second."

"What do you mean second? You won!"

"What about the Spanish guy?" Now I was completely confused.

"The Spanish guy? He punctured miles ago!"

"I can't believe it. I won?"

"Davis, you've won the stage! You won!"

"I can't believe it! I won!"

And that was the quote that went out on the wire, just as it was my mantra for the rest of the evening. I meant it literally. I was in disbelief. Echave had flatted twenty kilometers from the finish. The roads were densely lined with spectators, and we'd sped past without seeing him. No one in the break had noticed him; certainly, if we'd known we were racing for the win, it would've changed the dynamic of the group considerably. For my part, I would've tensed up, overthought it, and possibly blown it.

To the victor . . . after I'd collected a bouquet and a cool trophy (a solid silver silhouette of France, with diamonds embedded at that day's start and finish and a gold line connecting the two points), and some smooches from the podium girls, I had a moment with Paul Sherwen, a former pro rider now best known to Americans for his distinctive cycling commentary, alongside Phil Liggett, on the Versus network. Paul was still competing, but had ridden his seventh and final Tour the year before. He was covering this one for the BBC. There was a wistful look in his eye as he told me, "Mate, what you just did on the second day of your first Tour de France, I tried to do for seven bloody years."

Winning a Tour stage earns you some friends in that figurative pub I alluded to earlier. Not like in the *Cheers* bar, where everyone knows your name, but something better. I definitely earned a little more space, a tad more deference in the peloton.

I didn't need more respect in the '87 Tour, a year later. I needed one more stick of dynamite for the homestretch — needed to hold on to my top-end speed for another hundred meters. By then I'd earned a reputation as one of the top sprinters in the sport, and I was riding accordingly: holding my position in the mosh pit of the mass sprint, following the right wheels, jumping at just the right times. But my strength would always ebb in the final moments. I'd taken a third place one day, a fifth on another, but I was getting passed in the last seconds by badasses like Sean Kelly, the legendary Irishman, and the blazingly fast Dutchman Jean-Paul van Poppel.

In view of our early successes the previous year, 7-Eleven was having a disappointing Tour. Halfway through the race, we'd been shut out. Even by the harsh standards of the Grand Boucle, riders were suffering more than usual in this Tour. It was an intensely hot

July. By the midpoint of the race, we'd lost Bob Roll and Jeff Bradley to a dysentery-like affliction. I don't know that I'd ever seen Mike Neel, our director, quite so down.

On the drive to the hotel following a stage finish he blurted — his eyes doing that squinty thing they always did when he was serious — "One of you guys *really* needs to win a stage."

"When's the next sprinter's stage?" I asked, sitting shotgun in the team car.

"Stage 12," he answered. "Brive-la-Gaillarde to Bordeaux." The 228-kilometer push through the Aquitaine region ended with a two-lap circuit of downtown Bordeaux. We would ride 130 miles, then finish after a couple of laps on a tight circuit — a kind of criterium — my specialty back in the States.

"Well," I announced, "I'm going to win in Bordeaux."

I'd noticed it going back to the spring of 1981, when Connie and I drove around the West looking for races. If she did well, I tended to do well, for the simple reason that I didn't want to be known as Connie Carpenter's less talented boyfriend. Even if I *was* Connie Carpenter's less talented boyfriend. I responded well to external motivation. So here I was, calling my shot, jacking up the pressure on myself even though there are very few minutes in the Tour that aren't already pressure-packed. I'd had days in the Tour so tense that, upon completing them, I would ask the team masseur to pry my shoulders out of my ears, if you know what I mean. Five, six hours just clenching the handlebars, fighting for position, trying to stay out of the crashes, tended to tie one's muscles in knots.

Stage 12 that year was the opposite of one of those days. It felt like I was being guided by some unseen hand — an all-seeing velodeity whose beneficence did not extend to my rivals. I'm thinking in particular of Kelly, who went down in a crash while fighting for a bonus sprint. He remounted, suffered acutely for twenty minutes, then abandoned with a cracked collarbone. Sobbing, he was trundled onto an ambulance.

As we wended our way past vineyards and vast fields of sunflowers during the fifth hour of that day's stage, we settled into a pace that Jean-Claude Colotti found too desultory for his liking. The Frenchman attacked fifty kilometers from Bourdeaux, quickly building a lead of two and a half minutes. *Oh well,* I thought, *maybe it's not my day after all.*

As that thought crossed my mind, Van Poppel called his team-mates to the front and dropped the hammer. (He was defending his green "points" jersey, awarded to the Tour's best sprinter.) In short order, Jean-Claude was back among us, and I was back in the game.

Things got frantic and hectic on the run-in to the ancient city. But, unlike on so many other days, every time I got squeezed or bumped, *a lane would magically open elsewhere.* Once we got into Bordeaux proper, with its twisting, narrow streets, I was B'rer Rabbit in the briar patch, completely at ease and at home. I might as well have been contesting a criterium in Vail or Reno or Baltimore. Raúl Alcalá, our superb climbing and time trial specialist, led me through the two circuits, but, to be honest, my legs felt so good, I almost didn't need him. Rounding the final turn into the four-hundred-meter sprint to the finish, I stood on the pedals and called down the thunder. On the periphery of my vision, two riders fighting for position crashed against the barricade. I heard afterward that the pileup may have disrupted Van Poppel's sprint, but honestly, I don't think it mattered. There was no flagging of my power this afternoon: I was accelerating right up until the moment I crossed the line first, two bike-lengths ahead.

Where the win in Liévin felt a bit flukey—I had to be told that I'd won—this victory validated me. At least, in my mind. I'd called my shot, then backed it up in a stage that a lot of people expected me to do well in. Which is harder, if you think about it, than coming out of nowhere. That victory in Bordeaux opened the floodgates, in a sense, for 7-Eleven. Dag Otto won a stage in the Pyrenees, and Jeff Pierce won the final day in Paris. We were a powerful team, and I was the beneficiary of superb teamwork, although you'd never have known it, reading my rather self-absorbed re-marks to Susan Bickelhaupt of the *Boston Globe:*

> "Last year I was totally surprised, but this year I think a lot of people were looking for me to win," said Phinney, who was both panting and laughing at the finish line, and even broke into "Happy birthday to me!" at one point, in honor of his 28th birth-day three days ago. "What a great present to myself."

What a great present to myself!

Reading that now, from the remove of two-plus decades, I can't help thinking: *Is that guy just* begging *for the other shoe to drop, or what?* Let's just say my euphoria didn't last long. In this sport, it never does.

9

You're Not Supposed to See This

THERE IS THAT moment in *The Sun Also Rises* when Mike Campbell is asked how he lost his fortune. "Two ways," he replies. "Gradually, and then suddenly." That's a pretty fair description of my father's decline and demise.

After seven and a half years in remission, his PSA (prostate-specific antigen) level began a gradual rise, an ominous sign. By 1996, nine years after his diagnosis, the cancer in his prostate had returned, as had the metastasis in his right sit bone.

He countered with an experimental treatment that involved shutting down his adrenal glands. He went into partial remission for the next year and a half. When the cancer came back, he had run out of conventional therapy options.

Which did not stop him. Over the next two and a half years, he tried a handful of alternative treatments, during which time the bone "mets" continued to spread, until, by the spring of 2000 — just weeks after I'd been officially diagnosed with PD — he had more than twenty, plus soft-tissue cancer near the prostate and bladder, which necessitated the insertion of stents from his kidneys, to avoid kidney failure.

Things were looking bleak for Dad, but that spring, he found an alternative treatment — flaxseed oil mixed with cottage cheese —

that halted growth of the soft-tissue cancer and began to shrink his cancerous lymph nodes. He hooked up with the National Cancer Institute, and started an experimental protocol evaluating the chemo agent Taxotere, plus the anti-angiogenesis agent thalidomide. If he could just halt the growth of those bone mets, and if the flaxseed oil kept up its end of the bargain, hell, who knew? Gotta have hope, right?

The man was fighting for life. The last thing he needed to hear, I concluded, was the bad news that I was carrying around. My parents knew I'd been scheduling a lot of doctor appointments, trying to figure out what ailed me. They knew something was up.

The same way I tried to shield my children from the news, at first I soft-pedaled it to my parents. *The doctors say Parkinson's, but they say with medication I'll feel as good as I've ever felt for years to come!* Their concerns were not exactly allayed the morning I joined them for breakfast at the Chautauqua Dining Hall, a Boulder landmark at the foot of the Flatirons. As I repeatedly whiffed while trying to spear a piece of melon with my shaky left hand, a look of sadness crossed Damon's face. He glanced at my mother, as if to confirm his suspicions. I tried to make light of it:

"You guys weren't supposed to see that," I said jokingly.

Why try to hide the disease from my dad? Probably because I was, in a way, still hiding it from myself. A big part of me was in denial. I was only a few years removed from my last pro race. Yeah, I tripped now and again and shuffled along like a turtle on occasion and tired easily (truth be told, I was tired *all the time*). And there was that sporadic tremor, but hey, I still had days on the bike when I could tear people's legs off. I tried to convince myself that I would be the exception, that I was going to find a way out of, or around, this mess. This disease was not going to beat me. I wasn't gonna be that guy—the guy at the neurologist's office who could barely get out of his chair when the nurse called his name. That was not going to be me.

My pride, *my ego*, was all tied up in it. I was Thor, for crissakes — the God of Thunder! Hell, it had been only two years
since the 1998 Ride for the Roses, the annual fundraising weekend
for the Lance Armstrong Foundation. I was invited as a "celeb-
rity rider" for the mass-participation ride. Dad had been invited
for his work founding the Cyclists Combating Cancer website.
On the first night in Austin, we joined Lance at dinner with various sponsors, friends, and luminaries. I remember my father sitting between two famous riders, Sean Kelly and Miguel Indurain,
who'd won five straight Tours de France. Between Kelly's barely co-
herent brogue, Indurain's lack of English, and Damon being deaf
in one ear, there wasn't much of a conversation ongoing at their
end of the table. Although he was physically uncomfortable sitting
down through the long meal, Dad fairly beamed the entire evening, nonetheless. He was proud of his own role in Lance's fight.
That year, he showed up at the fledgling LAF headquarters, which
was a humble cottage just west of downtown, and asked the then-
CEO, Jeff Garvey, if he could help out in any way. Unaware of my
father's hearing impediment (unaware because Damon didn't tell
him), Jeff put him to work answering phones. (Eight years after
Damon died, I spoke at the ceremony when the new Livestrong
headquarters named a conference room after the website Damon
created for fellow cyclists.)

Dad was proud of his work on the CCC, and he was proud of
his son. He got to see me at the top of my game, on the bike, and
now, in the world. We rode together that weekend through the hot,
hilly hundred-miler, with me pacing him over the closing miles
along Highway 71 to the finish. He was zonked when we got back
to our hotel room, and promptly fell into a deep slumber.

As once he had watched his young son sleeping peacefully,
there I was listening to my old man softly snoring away. I reflected
on how lucky I was to have had this opportunity to be the man
he's always wanted me to be. An old memory came to mind. I was

eleven years old and playing baseball in Little League. We had a good team and I was leading our league in home runs, having averaged one per game the entire season. Dad had yet to see me play but finally made it to a makeup game. I was primed to show him just what he'd been missing. Unfortunately the umpire didn't show and so the coaches asked for a volunteer. My heart went into my throat as my father stood up and said he would take them up on it. *No! Not Dad!* I shouted out in my head. *This'll ruin everything!* And I came unglued as inning after inning went by with each at-bat going worse than the last. I was so self-conscious in front of him, trying so hard to *mash* the ball, and so acutely sensitive to his called strikes . . . it was a nightmare and I hated him for being there, hated him for making me feel like a poser on that baseball diamond.

We may have had our issues over the years, but I loved the man who lay curled up in the next bed. He had become my go-to guy as I grew into a father myself. Two years later, it crushed me, the idea of his witnessing my strength, my vitality, ebbing prematurely away.

I didn't want to add to his woes. Because he had problems much worse than mine. By the spring of 2001, he was in sharp decline. As the cancer infiltrated his spine, he was given Decadron, a strong steroid that gave him such an extreme (but temporary) burst of vitality that he went charging up Green Mountain in two hours—a hike he hadn't attempted in years. While the Decadron sparked him for a short time, it also made him delusional and insomniac.

Quite suddenly, it seemed, he was reduced to sitting around the house in nothing but an adult diaper, to protect the furniture against his worsening incontinence. My mother referred to him as "Gandhi." None of us—not me, not Mom, not Alice—were coping well with his sad new reality. We had been reduced to a kind of paralysis.

Much of the crisis was managed by the woman who, from all appearances, should have had the least time or energy to deal with it. Connie was the mother of two young children, running a business and ministering to a husband with a chronic disease. Now she stepped into the void to ease the suffering of my father, with whom she always shared a deep, mutual affection and respect. "I'm honored to help you, Damon," she told him. "Just let me."

It was Connie who talked my father into checking himself into the emergency room, in order to begin the process of weaning him off the various meds he was taking. It was Connie who donned a telephone headset and sat for hours, navigating the mystifying labyrinth of Kaiser health care.

And it was Connie, finally, along with an emergency room doctor who worked with my father over several visits, who helped him understand that it was time to set aside "life-saving" treatments. It was time to make him as comfortable as possible, and let the cancer take its course.

Ever the pragmatist, my dad cut to the chase that day in Boulder Community Hospital. He agreed that hospice care was his best option. "You may not want to hear this," he told us, "but I'm not afraid of death, or of dying." And yet, he could not give it a free pass. He was constitutionally incapable. Even after moving into hospice — where the whole point was to let go — he dug in as if he were defending the Alamo. He clung to life for months. One day he fell, injuring his hip. The nurses were afraid he'd broken it. To keep him from leaving his bed without first summoning them, they tethered him to it — one more withdrawal from his dwindling store of dignity. The man was so ready to die, but could not. He contemplated suicide, but rejected the idea, worried about the effect it might have on the cancer community.

On his good days I'd rescue him from hospice, driving him into the mountains he'd so loved to climb on his bike. We ate pancakes at the Wondervu Café, nearly nine thousand feet above sea level, high above the plains and at the doorstep of the high peaks. Over breakfast the stories flowed. Dad remembered driving the family to skate at nearby Lake Pactola, when Alice and I were around seven and five years old, respectively. I was throwing a fit, as the lumpy windswept ice was tough to handle on my twin-bladed kiddie skates — until Dad suggested I try pushing an old folding chair along the ice to stay in balance. And it worked! At least until I got cocky and sprinted into an ice rut, whereby the chair stopped cold and I went flying, cracking my noggin hard, after which my wailing could be heard halfway to Denver.

We reminisced about another outing, when I was a little older. Dad and I drove up past Wondervu to the east portal of the Moffat Tunnel (a railway passage that cuts through the Continental Divide) for a Nordic adventure. We skied some miles up to the base of Rogers Pass, where there was a tiny hut. We'd brought along Cassidy, our intrepid collie, and on the way back down I'd almost peed my pants laughing at the sight of my father careening along in an overly wide-track stance, the dog barking wildly while running full speed between his legs, the entire descent of the steep, narrow trail.

They make a mean homemade pie at the Wondervu Café, and on his every bike ride through, Dad would never fail to stop for a cup of coffee and a piece of apple pie. That was his payoff, his reward, beyond the satisfaction of adding to his mileage log. This particular stretch of alpine roadway was used as a principal climb in the Boulder Mountain road race — the original "Queen" stage in the Red Zinger/Coors Classic. I recalled how one year a few of us had been stopped at a railroad crossing after getting dropped on the climb. With no train in sight, an argument ensued as to whether we should duck under the crossing gates and risk getting DQ'd from the race (but catch up to the next group of riders just ahead, who had got through cleanly), or not. While a couple of guys went for it (and escaped sanction — or worse, being flattened by the oncoming train), I'd surprised myself by hanging back. This from the guy who, as a kid, fearlessly dashed across many a busy street — absolutely certain he could outrace the oncoming cars — much to my father's chagrin. Dad smiled at the story, saying simply that I'd done the right thing.

Three weeks before he died, we drove west up Lefthand Canyon to Brainard Lake, hard by the Indian Peaks Wilderness at ten thousand feet of elevation. Both of us had huffed our way up there many times on bicycles. As a family, we'd backpacked throughout this range, and more recently, my father would lug his precious Hasselblad camera gear up there at o-dark-hundred, waiting for the beautiful first light to illuminate the mountains.

Querencia is a Spanish word for the place one feels most at home. These mountains, like the Alps, like the Dolomites, served as such a home for my father. He was too weak to walk far from the car that day. But he was happy. It was the last time he made it up into the mountains, and the last time I saw pure contentment in his eyes.

He always put on a brave face — all those decades of stoicism had prepared him well. After a family visit to the hospice one afternoon, we took our leave, but I realized I had left some item — a jacket? — in his room. When I went back to get it, he was alone and sobbing.

"You're not supposed to see this," he told me through his tears. He'd held cancer at bay for thirteen-plus years, and for much of that time he'd had an upbeat demeanor and ready smile. But a wave of sadness at seeing Kelsey and Taylor had overcome him.

"God*dammit!*" he declared. "I wanted to see my grandchildren grow up."

On the last night of his life, the family gathered round and bid him goodnight. Connie and I hung around a little while longer to set his beloved Mozart on continuous play, and I leaned in to give him what would be a final kiss. "I love you, Dad!" I said, starting to cry. "I love you, Dave." Then he added, "I'm going to sleep now, and I'm going to dream of the Alpe d'Huez."

He passed just as the sun cracked the horizon, the morning sky a rich luminous red, his favorite time of day. Morning light. Perfect light.

Railing a turn, while wearing the sprint leader's jersey, at the 1986 Coors Classic. In all, I won twenty-two stages of this race.

Winning my second stage of the Tour de France, in Bordeaux, 1987. A sprinter's dream.

A week after she won gold in the women's road race, Connie wishes me luck before the team time trial at the 1984 Olympics. Ron Kiefel, Roy Knickman, Andy Weaver, and I took the bronze.

Riding alongside Wookie, my friend and wingman, at the 1990 Tour de France, just days after Taylor was born.

On the podium in Bordeaux at the 1987 Tour de France. It doesn't get much sweeter than this.

Moments after slicing my face to ribbons during the 1988 Liège–Bastogne–Liège race. IsoGlass is tempered safety glass. I found out the hard way that the rear windshield of its team car was not, in fact, equipped with IsoGlass.

John Kelly

Cruising on the tandem with Taylor—he's the one in soccer cleats. Even at the age of six, he wanted to go faster.

Damon, Taylor, and Davis—three generations of Phinney boys. I treasure this picture.

John Kelly

Interviewing George Hincapie for OLN at the 1998 Paris–Roubaix race. Parkinson's cut short my television career.

Hanging with the fam on the back porch in Boulder, 2008.

Above: Trying to stay calm during brain surgery.

Left: Post-surgery, with thirty-five staples in my skull and "Bob" stitched into my chest. When doctors flipped the switch, I hoped to be a new man.

Davis Phinney

Frank Matson/Citizen Pictures

Robert Beck

Taylor smoking the velodrome at the 2008 Beijing Olympics, en route to seventh place. His peak was still six months away.

Robert Beck

Left: Cheering for Taylor at the Laoshan Velodrome, outside Beijing. Keeping it positive and upbeat . . . for the camera.

Below: Lance Armstrong enjoys a few laughs with Taylor and me at the 2008 Ride for the Roses.

Elizabeth Kreutz

Wan Tu

Here I am receiving a Coca-Cola Award during the Beijing Games, in recognition of my work with the Davis Phinney Foundation.

Taylor throws his arms wide after winning a stage of Le Triptyque des Monts et Châteaux, less than a month after winning his second World Championship title on the track.

Out on a training ride with Taylor. We have our best talks on the bike.

10

If God Were a Cyclist . . .

LOVE BOULDER, LOVE coming home to Boulder, will perhaps always live in Boulder. Yet there came a time, in the months after my diagnosis, that I wanted—needed—to get out of Boulder. A big part of my identity had been tied up in being exceptionally strong and vital, yet there I was, trembling as I walked down the street. The word was out that I was ill, and every time I went out in public, I felt people's eyes on me. In hindsight, I'm sure the sense of being scrutinized was largely in my head, but that didn't diminish my desire to *escape,* to go somewhere nobody knew me, to de-stress and decompress while I figured out my new identity.

Seven months before my father died, Connie and I spent a glorious week performing a reconnaissance of the jagged peaks of the Dolomites, our tour highlighted by an area known as the Alta Badia and the town of Corvara, of which Damon had always said, "If God were a cyclist, he'd live here." It was an unlikely statement from a man who professed to be an atheist, but we found truth in those words. For me, nature is the best sanctuary, and my spirituality—my sense of who I am—is best expressed in the mountains.

For years Connie and I had been holding our Bike Camps in Tuscany. While our clients enjoyed themselves and often repeated camps with us, many also expressed an interest in riding more mountainous terrain than could be found around our Tuscan home base in Castagneto Carducci.

During that blessed week in the Dolomiti, I found myself nearly asymptomatic for the first time in memory. Why? Maybe it was the clean mountain air of the Alta Badia region, the mystical beauty of those natural spires. Maybe God really did live here, Connie and I mused. Whatever it was, I wished I could bottle it. We launched our Bike Camp there the following year.

From Corvara we made our way south to Asolo, an exquisite medieval town in the foothills of the Dolomites, in the neighboring Veneto region. Our friend Lennard Zinn, a technical writer for *VeloNews,* could do his job from anywhere. So he, his wife, Sonny, and their two young daughters had pulled up stakes and moved to Asolo for a year, to travel, absorb the culture, and share an adventure. One of my memories from that trip is of a nocturnal hike with the Zinns to the castle high above Asolo, and the sight of young Emily Zinn reciting lines from *King Lear* under the light of the full moon. Later, Lennard spoke eloquently about what a gift it had been to spend extended time with his children. Connie and I longed to share a similar adventure, to give our family — and ourselves — such a gift.

"We are meant to do this," she declared. But at the time, there was no way. We couldn't abandon my father in his hour of greatest need.

Damon died not quite six weeks after the 2001 terrorist attacks. As seven-year-old Kelsey breathlessly declared after school the day of September 11, "The world trading posts were taken out! I'm glad we don't have any trading posts around here."

The country was galvanized in the weeks and months after 9/11 in a way it has not been since. But beneath the calls for unity and patriotism, there arose a discourse of fear and mistrust — an atmosphere that, to be honest, made it easier for us to contemplate a move out of the country.

Connie returned to the Veneto the following spring. It was near the city of Bassano del Grappa that she met the bright and vibrant Francesca Eger, director of the English International School in nearby Rosà. Connie got an immediate good feeling about Francesca and the school, whose focus was for Italian children to learn English. While Taylor and Kelsey would have an advantage for half their class load, they would be immersed in Italian for the other half as well as most of their free time.

Through the Zinns, we met Steve and Krista Smith. Though she barely knew us, Krista worked tirelessly to help us find a place to live. We finally landed a house outside nearby Marostica, an ancient walled city that sits with its back to the Altopiano ("high plain") of Asiago, a rugged, breathtaking plateau ringed by Dolomites in three directions. In this way, it reminded us of Boulder.

By this time Taylor was twelve, Kelsey, eight. Both of them had been to Italy several times, for family vacations or our Bike Camps. So they had a certain comfort level with the idea of living there. But it was still a scary prospect. Connie and I smiled at their disparate concerns about their future classmates:

Him: "What if they don't like me?"

Her: "What if I don't like them?"

And so the morning arrived in August 2002 when we left Boulder with seven suitcases and one double-bike case. We arrived in Marostica the following day, hungry, cranky, and catatonic with jet lag. After checking in to our temporary oasis, a lovely ten-room inn called the Due Mori, we ate dinner, then crashed, boys in one room, girls in another. After what happened on our first night in Italy, we damn near turned around and went home.

Sometime in the small hours, Connie was awakened by Kelsey, who was writhing and flailing in her bed, her mouth clenched, her eyes eerily wide open. She was having a seizure. Connie called the police — it still boggles my mind that she had the local emergency number committed to memory — and asked for an ambulance. Then she lifted Kelsey, whose body remained disturbingly rigid, carried her down two flights of stairs, and placed her on a sofa in the lobby.

The lobby was soon transformed into a Felliniesque scrum of humanity: Connie in a pair of boxers and a T-shirt; a waitress from the restaurant, who was cooing gently in Kelsey's ear when she came to; the innkeepers, the police, and, not long after, paramedics. Thus, on our first night in Marostica, did we find ourselves in the back of an ambulance, en route to a hospital in Bassano. Connie and Kelsey spent the night in the pediatric wing. The doctors did some tests on Kels the next day and found nothing immediately pressing. But it was a scary and inauspicious beginning to our trip. (Kelsey was later diagnosed with benign rolandic seizure disorder, which remits at puberty.)

I have never stopped flashing back to the sight of Connie with Kelsey in her arms. It says everything about how we got through—and are still getting through—a truly difficult time. Despite our differences, or perhaps because of them, Connie and I had long balanced each other. In our home and at our camps, we'd always been equal partners. But my Parkinson's had unbalanced the equation. In many ways, I'd become a burden, an anchor to my oh-so-strong wife, whom our friends had long since nicknamed "Broad-shouldered Connie." When she scooped up Kelsey in her arms that night, Connie was already carrying me.

It was Taylor who crossed the ocean with the biggest bundle of anxiety, who was most worried about moving halfway across the world and starting a new school where they spoke a different language. And it was Taylor, naturally, who made the most effortless transition. Within a few days after we'd arrived, he started practicing with the local *calcio* (soccer) club, and was immediately embraced. His new friends didn't know or care that his parents had won some bike races back in the day. They were only interested in the fact that he had speed to burn, a hard, accurate shot, and a knack for converting breakaways into goals.

It almost felt like cheating. Right away, we were accepted into this community.

Well, maybe not right away. It's not like these other soccer families were inviting us to their homes for dinner. They were friendly, but understandably leery. Before they knew my story, some of the other dads would see me tremoring, would hear my slurred speech, and assume—perhaps—that I'd been drinking. To their credit, once they learned my story and found out I had a disability, they began to look out for me and care for me in an understated, unselfconscious way that, to be honest, blew me away.

Taylor had joined the century-old Union Sportiva Marosticense, the local soccer club, which meant that our whole family had joined. For the rare far-flung tournaments, the team hired a bus and we traveled in a distinctly Italian fashion. Every two hours or so we would pull off the autostrada and everyone would pile out. With practiced efficiency, the adults would set up little card tables, drape tablecloths over them, and unpack the provender: salami and cheeses and loaves of crusty bread, paired with hearty wines from the region.

When we arrived at the stadium, one of the other dads would, without fail, link his arm in mine and escort me through the parking lot. Inevitably, we'd head straight to the nearest café, where they made sure I had a place to sit, then I'd be handed an espresso. No fuss, no fanfare, no big deal, just a patient paternalism that touched me to the core.

It was almost amusing to watch their faces as we attempted to explain why we'd moved from America to what we considered their little corner of paradise. A commonly expressed sentiment was: "Why would you come here? Your grandparents are not from here." And the all-important query: "How could you leave your church?" In this part of Italy, God and family were everything. It mattered very much to some people where you were from, and how many centuries your ancestors had lived there. A regional political party called the Lega Nord had long advocated for greater autonomy from the federal government, and, at times secession. So just as we were welcomed, we were never allowed to forget that we were *stranièri* — foreigners.

Almost never. At home on Via Boscaglie, we were surrounded by friends. On the first night in our new home, we heard a blessed, welcome voice — in English! — asking if there was anything we needed. This was our kindly neighbor Mara Salvini, who was born in South America but raised in Italy. She was a godsend, especially for Kelsey, who spent many days helping Mara around the house and chasing after her two little ones.

On the other side of us lived the Parise family, whose padrone, Gianni, was the brother of our landlord. His wife, Daniela, proved to be so generous and kind, delivering advice and home-cooked food in equal measure, that we came to nickname her Saint Daniela. Showing us slightly less affection was Daniela's mother-in-law — La Nonna, as we called her — whose little apartment faced our house. The Nonna's mantra was "Non sento niente, non vedo niente": I can't hear anything, I can't see anything. And yet we found her to be a formidable watchdog, an all-seeing presence who missed very little of what went on across the driveway.

As the ultimate proof of her kindness, Saint Daniela accompanied us to the Questura, the police station in nearby Vicenza, an oppressive, bureaucratic purgatory into which we were forced to descend to acquire, then renew annually, our visas, or *permessi di soggiorno* — permission to stay. In the Questura, we were herded into what amounted to a holding pen, along with a hundred or so other anxious *stranièri*: North Africans, eastern Europeans, a smattering of Americans. Once there, we would wait and wait some more, until it was our turn to go bowing and scraping before some expressionless bureaucrat behind one of the thick bullet-proof windows. Had he lived long enough to experience the Questura, Dante would almost surely have added a tenth circle of hell to his Inferno.

It was their job to find some fault, to manufacture some pretext, however thin and unreasonable, to refuse our application, to demand more documentation, to get us to cough up more fees, to get us back to the Questura. A tense, fearful vibe permeated the building. I truly hated going there. After two hours in that place, I'd be shaking like the subwoofer in Snoop Dogg's Escalade.

Our reward for enduring the Questura, for outlasting those *stronzi* (assholes), was the privilege of legally living *la dolce vita* for another year. There is a rhythm and flow to life in Italia, and despite occasional frustration, it was our pleasure to find that rhythm. We lived just a kilometer or so outside Marostica, down a country lane lined with vineyards. Our backyard abutted a cornfield. To the west, a stand of cherry trees had been planted. Marostica is best known for two things: its sweet, flavorful heart-shaped *ciliègie*—cherries—and for the enormous marble chessboard covering its town square, the Piazza degli Scacchi.

The hills bunching up behind the town feature hopeful church steeples, carefully tended shrines, perfectly spaced stands of trees. I never tired of taking in the blunt majesty of Monte Grappa, or the wide, rushing Brenta River cleaving it from the Altopiano.

I have idealized, airbrushed memories of that time, because we really did slow down the tempo of our lives. I'd like to say it was by choice—to live more like the locals. The truth was, we had to. I was struggling as never before.

My Parkinson's had moved into the passing lane; my tremor was more pronounced and stubborn than ever. Turning over twenty or thirty times a night, with renewed shaking at every turn, cut deeply into my sleep. Even in the still of night, PD had me. Having experimented with a variety of drugs during that first year after my diagnosis, I'd gone off almost all of them. I was, as my doctors put it, "undermedicated." That was by design. My initial experience with PD meds was that they either had no effect on me or their side effects were as bad as, or worse than, the disease itself. (While on a drug called Mirapex I would rise, eat breakfast, drink coffee . . . then hit a coma-like wall, frequently requiring a four-hour nap. Next.)

If I was coming to pieces, I wanted to bear witness to my own degeneration—I wanted to know where I was, without the complicating, fogging effects of a potpourri of pills.

And so I shook. I mean, I was all over the place, like a figurine in one of those old vibrating electric-football games. I pitched in where possible. I drove the kids home from school even though that wasn't always a great idea. When my left hand got really shaky, which was basically every time I tried to use it, I steered with my right—except when I needed that hand to shift the car, an exercise complicated by the fact that my left leg, my clutch leg, also had obedience issues, leaving me no choice sometimes but to stab at the clutch pedal with my foot. It made for some herky-jerky rides, and although I know the kids definitely noticed, they never complained.

A simple trip to the grocery store entailed in-depth planning. First I scoped out where I was going to park. Upon exiting the car, my left hand went immediately into a pocket of my carefully chosen pants or jacket. In my *right* pants pocket was a coin I would use to rent a cart, which then gave me a place to anchor the left hand. Depending on the season, and my wardrobe, I might keep my wallet in my back right pocket, or on the left-side, inside breast pocket of my jacket. It was like Ike getting ready for D-day, and all to make sure I didn't have a public shake-fest in the checkout lane. Honestly, sometimes the highlight of my day was an afternoon nap, or channel surfing with a canister of Pringles (yes, really) and a tall beer after everyone had gone to sleep. Sprawled on the floor, left hand tucked under my bum, leaning back on the couch. That was my pose. I welcomed *any* opportunity to forget—or briefly escape—this damn disease.

I still went for walks, checked out the farmers' market, took hikes and s-l-o-o-o-w bike rides. There were days I could barely go fast enough to keep from tipping over. And on those days I celebrated . . . not tipping over.

I approached life with Parkinson's the way I'd approached it as a sprinter. I weathered the bad days, tolerated them, hunkered down and got through them in the knowledge that there was a good day out there, a day with my name on it. There was a stage coming up (had to be!) with smallish mountains (or none at all!). There was a course coming up with a technical finish that suited me (possibly tomorrow!). Because unless your name is Eddy Merckx or Lance Armstrong or Connie Carpenter, you know the deal going in: even when you're feeling flash and digging deep into your suitcase of courage (to borrow from the inimitable Sherwen), you go into every race with the understanding that you fail far more often than not. But you don't let the defeats grind you down. And if you keep your head in the game, if you don't let the losses eat you alive, you end up learning from them. And eventually, you learn enough to reach the line first and throw your hands in the air.

11

For a Little While, I Was Cured

WINNING A RACE and pointing both hands at the sky was always a transcendent moment for me, a distillation of triumph and joy and relief that I liken to plugging yourself into the current of the earth itself. And while victory is transient, that feeling can be accessed over and over again. I'm no longer in search of major victories, but daily victories. That is what sustains me.

On a smaller but still-rewarding scale, photography gives me a similar pleasure. I began to pursue it seriously in Italy. That country offered such a daily visual feast that Connie was constantly moved to paint (she is a gifted watercolorist with a uniquely whimsical style), just as I found myself getting more and more excited about simply taking pictures. I definitely didn't break the bank on equipment. Where Damon had favored a bulky Hasselblad camera (the kind Ansel Adams used), which took ultra-high-quality images on large-format negatives, I was content with my first-generation Canon Elph point-and-shoot. As Damon himself used to say, the best camera is the one you have with you.

By capturing these images, I was able to safeguard a bit of the joy from the moment of discovery. One Sunday early in our stay in

Italy, all four of us went exploring on our town bikes, with no particular destination in mind. We ended up on some back road in the hills between Marostica and Bassano. It was autumn, and the farmers were burning their organic refuse. The haze and smoke gave the light a certain . . . density. We pedaled past Palladian villas whose statues stared imperiously down on us. Everything looked like a postcard—the vineyards, the fallow fields, and the gnarled forms of olive trees. I couldn't put the camera away. To this day, those images evoke a sense of place; they preserve memories that might otherwise have dissolved. I didn't realize it then, but I was discovering a way to fight back against Parkinson's. I was laying the groundwork for the strategy that guides me to this day.

I was training myself to be on the lookout for certain fleeting moments. After a while, I realized that I was doing it, exercising that watchfulness, whether I was carrying a camera or not. By stockpiling these snapshots, literal and figurative—a smile from the cute barista with the provocative tattoo, a sunrise over Monte Grappa—I could lose myself in them.

That discovery made all the difference for me in Italy, and over the years that followed. It was there, with the camera at first and then without it, that I realized I could transform the tenor of a day by going through it with my eyes, and mind, wide open: by consciously taking note of, and appreciating, the small victories and minor grace notes available to us all.

In those instants, fleeting though they often were, I forgot to be self-conscious, forgot to worry about the future, forgot about the disease. Which is another way of saying that, for a little while, I was cured.

My children are a rich source of these "curative moments," these daily victories. Taylor had been playing soccer for a year when Kelsey the Brave, as I nicknamed her, decided to try out for the Marosticense's under-ten team. This took particular courage, considering that there was no girls' team, but she was determined to play. She took heart from another pioneering female, Gloria, an older girl who played on one of the boys' squads. La Gloria.

In the locker room on the first day of tryouts, the boys stood a short distance away, gaping at Kelsey as if she were a zoo animal, talking about her but not to her. Taylor, at my request, went in with her. Quickly sizing up the situation, he said loudly, and in the local dialect, in order to be perfectly understood, "This is my sister, be nice to her . . . or else!" T had become an icon to the younger boys, and it helped to have him lend his support.

Kelsey's first coach—the "mister," as Italians call their soccer coaches—was an elderly man with a granddaughter her age, and he took care of her, kept an eye on her and treated her fairly. While the boys roughhoused and goofed off, Kelsey hung on his every word, answering "Si, mister." Nor did it hurt that she was, and is, a very good athlete. She played defense, and often earned the coveted numeral 2, the uniform worn by the team's top defender.

The coach grew to rely on her and to trust her. In a game against a powerhouse opponent, a player on the other side was called for a foul. Marostica was awarded a penalty kick. Up to the ball strode our gifted striker, a supremely confident boy named Manuel, who was taken aback—along with a number of parents—when the coach said, "No. I want Kelsey."

Looking at my daughter in that excruciating moment, I saw her gulp and take a deep breath. She stood just behind the ball, stepped back, then drilled a shot into the upper right-hand corner. The goalie never had a chance. Around us, the other parents cried out, "Brava!"—as distinct from the masculine form of that word, *bravo*. *Brava!* I still love the sound of that word.

At the end of his second season with US Marosticense, Taylor also found himself staring down a high-pressure kick. In his first few months with the club, he'd made up for his lack of Italian by learning as many profanities as he could. He didn't know what

they meant; he just knew they made his teammates laugh when he
shouted them in the locker room.

By his second season, he'd learned enough Italian to retire
the blue language. And he had enough confidence in his skills to
sculpt his hair into a version of the "faux hawk" made famous by
soccer superstar David Beckham. Taylor backed it up by putting in
some serious hours on the practice pitch and in the backyard. By
putting topspin and sidespin on the ball, he became adept at curl-
ing shots over the clothesline — the "wall" of defenders consisting,
in this case, of towels clothespinned to the rope — and into the up-
per-right corner of the net, after which we would all carry on and
shout, "Go-o-o-o-a-a-a-l-l-l-l!"

In the crucial moments of the final game, with a giant trophy
on the line for his team, Taylor was chosen to take the shot he'd
been simulating in the backyard. "Oh my God," I said to Connie.
"He's practiced this exact shot a hundred times this week!"

Loping toward the ball at a forty-five-degree angle, he planted
his left foot hard, his right leg swinging through like a cracking
whip. We watched the ball arc itself perfectly up and just over the
"wall" and embed itself in the upper right-hand corner of the net.
On the field and in the bleachers, the Marosticense went nuts.
The kid had bent it like Beckham! Afterward, he was hoisted on
the shoulders of his teammates. We have a framed picture of that
scene, which, along with Kelsey's similar heroics, were two of our
sweetest moments in Italy. Certainly it was the apex of Taylor's
soccer "career."

By establishing his identity as a soccer player, Taylor created a
kind of refuge for himself. He didn't have to answer the question
Why aren't you racing a bicycle? Because the answer was obvious:
he was all about *calcio*. So what if his father had won stages of the
Tour de France? So what if his mother was an Olympic gold medalist whose jersey hung in the church of the Madonna del Ghisallo,
a famous shrine to cycling north of Milan? Taylor was blazing his
own path.

In this way, he created space for himself to have fun on his bicycle. When we took a ride in Italy, it was an exploration, an adventure. It wasn't a workout. "We'd generally go out for an hour, hour and a half," he recalled for a reporter in 2009. "Not that long, but long enough to trigger some endorphins. I thought that's how it was going to feel all the time. That has not proven to always be the case."

One afternoon not long after we'd moved to Italy, T and I headed out for a ride to a tiny village partway up the Altopiano. I prided myself on finding the least traveled roads, which sounds nice in theory. Small roads = more fun, bigger adventure, right? Not always. In this case, the road was less traveled because it went straight up the hillside. The steepest sections featured horizontal grooves, designed to give tractors better traction as they chugged their way up. It was a road made for farm equipment, not twelve-year-old boys.

The hill kicked my butt, and I had roughly three times the power I do now. Taylor was miserable, but hung in there, dropping down into his lowest gear, gritting his teeth, and weaving his way up wherever possible.

We finally reached the village, and I apologized as he recovered in silence. When he finally spoke, though, he wasn't upset. "Halfway up, I was hating life," he told me. "I was asking myself, 'Why am I doing this?' I wanted to quit. But you were up ahead, so I figured I might as well keep going. But now that I'm up here, I'm psyched and so happy that I made it — and I realize that there's nowhere else I'd rather be than right here, with you."

When I was twelve, our family went on a three-day, twenty-six-mile backpacking trip around Mount Audubon, in the Indian Peaks Wilderness Area of Colorado. One evening, after a disagreement with my mother, my dad set out on a hike up to Buchanan Pass. I went with him. Determined to reach the summit before sunset, he set an urgent, challenging pace. But I was coming up on my thirteenth birthday and beginning to discover my own strength. I stayed right with him. Several times he looked back, to check on my progress, and was surprised to find me right on his heels. We made it to the top in time to take in a dramatic sunset on the Continental Divide. It was one of those rare moments when he told me, straight up, that he was impressed, and proud of me. I savored those words more than that spectacular sunset.

Three decades later, on a different mountain on a different continent, I looked across at my own twelve-year-old son, bedraggled but happy, proud of himself because he knew that I was proud of him. The difference between the twelve-year-old Taylor and the twelve-year-old version of me was that he felt my pride in him, and heard me express it almost every day of his life. Before either of my children had so much as been conceived, I vowed that I would always be emotionally available to them, embrace them when they needed it.

Toward the end of eighth grade, Taylor needed a lot of reassurance. "I was a stressed little cookie," he recalls of that time. To graduate from middle school in Italy, students must pass an exam that involves the execution of a complex project. After selecting a geographic region (T chose Vietnam), the aspiring high-schoolers are required to write about it in depth, tying in all they'd learned in math, language, history, science, art, and geography. After that, students must give an oral presentation — in Italian — summarizing their findings before an "interrogation committee" of teachers. A lot of kids fail and are forced to repeat the eighth grade. Following an intensive period of study and tutoring (thanks especially to our neighbors, the Parises!), Taylor passed. But the experience left him so traumatized, he's since confided, that the pressure of competing in the Olympics or defending a world title just ain't no big thing. I've heard him tell reporters, "I left all my stress in eighth grade."

. . .

One year in Marostica had slipped into a second. While this *dolce vita* stripped much of the stress from my life, it also began to feel, at times, as if I'd entered the Witness Protection Program. I had disappeared. It fed my gnawing fear that everything I had to offer the world had already been offered — that my remaining years would be a long, slow, tremulous fade to black. I felt prematurely . . . ancient. And quite often, invisible.

Two and a half years after my diagnosis, I'd come to terms with the fact that I had Parkinson's. I'd also begun to form a rough strategy for how I would push back against it, how I could improve the quality of my life despite having to share it with this interloper. Encouraged by Lance Armstrong's Livestrong example, I felt that I, too, could awaken and inspire people with my message of hope. First I had to fine-tune that message, and gain a bit of confidence in my ability to deliver it. In February of 2003, I got that chance.

I'd been invited to accept a "legends" trophy and give a short speech at the 2003 Endurance Sports Awards banquet in California, a kind of Oscars for the lean and fit set, a gathering of leg-shaving men and women more comfortable in Lycra and unitards than they are in formal attire. The guy running the show was my old friend Bob Babbitt, cofounder of Competitor Publishing, who also happens to be one of the people who popularized the triathlon in this country. Since 1980, when he showed up at the Hawaii Ironman on a bike with a fuzzy raccoon seat cover, solid rubber tires, and a boom box taped to the handlebars, the Ironman brand has gone global: its scores of events around the world now sell out in roughly ninety seconds. A born storyteller and closet ham, he runs the Las Vegas Rock 'n' Roll Marathon in full Elvis regalia, and dresses up as a green frog for the Columbia Muddy Buddy Ride and Run, a popular series he founded. ("Once you go green," he's been known to inform distaff competitors, "you never go back.")

As it happens, Babbitt is also a notorious softy. The Challenged Athletes Foundation, which he started in 1997, has raised $30 million to provide grants and sports-specific prosthetics for competitors with physical challenges.

I flew in from Italy the day before the event, which was held at Sea World in San Diego. I'd been on training rides with many of the triathletes in attendance, back in the day in Boulder, so my comfort level going in was pretty solid. Indeed, I felt so comfortable during cocktails that I struck up a conversation with a guy who looked *really* familiar, even though I couldn't put my finger on where we'd met before.

"Do I know you?" I asked. "'Cause you look very familiar."

"Umm, *maybe*," replied the actor Will Ferrell, who was then supremely gracious when I fell all over myself apologizing upon realizing who he was.

Before introducing me, Bob played a highlight reel of me winning half a dozen races. There I was, looking buff and vital and predatory, snatching victory after victory, each time thrusting my arms up into that familiar, uppercase *V*.

The contrast was stark between that two-wheeled warrior and the man who then made his halting, uncertain way onto the stage. I noted that, like that bike racer on the big screen, Babbitt's androgynous trophies depicted a competitor with arms upraised.

I urged the audience to raise its arms in triumph at every opportunity. "Like when your toast comes up and it's not burnt. *Yesss!*" Up went my arms, and as a wave of laughter from the audience washed over me, I knew everything was going to work out just fine.

While my voice was steady and calm, my tremor was in full plumage, so much so that whenever my body came in contact with the Plexiglas lectern, it shook. That, in turn, made the twin slender microphones wobble crazily, their round heads calling to mind a pair of buzzing insects.

"God, these are like bugs!" I exclaimed, interrupting myself at one point. "We need Bug Off! to attack these microphones."

While that line got big laughs, it didn't stop the microphones from wobbling. So Babbitt and his cohost, Ironman announcer Mike Reilly, flanked me, holding them steady. "Cycling is a team sport," I noted, and internally I registered how accepting I was of their help. It had taken me a while to get to this point, this acceptance.

Clutching the ESA's foot-high statuette in my right hand, I made the point to the aerobic legends assembled before me that, early in my racing career, I was short on endurance. "I was fast, I wanted to get done with everything really quickly and thrust my arms in the air. What I learned from years of doing long races and long hard training sessions was key: patience. To be successful, I had to put the proper time into preparation, to respect the process."

Now that I had PD, I told them, "I'm forced to have tremendous patience to do the simplest things." My friend Paul Huddle had buttoned the top button on my shirt before the banquet, I noted, "because my hands don't work as well anymore." Simple truth, but when was I so willing to admit it?

I wasn't looking for pity. If anything, I said, "I feel very strong in where I am with this disease because of my background, and what I was able to accomplish in cycling."

Where I felt blessed to be an athlete, "I almost feel more fortunate now, because I'm able to find new ways to express myself that aren't just through my physical capability."

If I was still casting about, in my private life, to find the exact forms that expression would take, well, the audience didn't need to know that. But there was one message I did want them to hear:

Whether it was the smile of a child or a great training ride or, in my case, the toast popping up unburnt, I told the audience, every day yields a score of small victories. When you recognize one of those in your own life, "Give it one of these." Up went my arms.

I shared a conversation I'd had with Kelsey a few days earlier. When I told her I was going to America to receive an award, she asked me, "Daddy, are you going to get in the hall of fame, like Mommy?" (Between the Olympic Hall of Fame and various cycling, skating, rowing, and school-related halls, Connie has lost track of the number of halls of fame into which she's been inducted.)

"No, sweetie," I told Kelsey. "But this banquet is a big deal. You'll see. I'll bring back pictures."

I then pointed a camcorder at the crowd, as if to say, Let's show her what a big deal it is. Next came this roaring cheer, as people rose from their seats and struck the pose du jour: that uppercase *V*. With the camcorder in my right hand, I joined them. It was worth the trip across the ocean, to live that moment.

The reaction to my message convinced me that I had something to say, something to offer. And I liked being onstage, feeling alive. After that evening at Sea World, I grew firmer in my conviction that I was meant to do something other than drop out and hide behind a disease. I had begun to discern a larger purpose for my life. This was no small victory.

12

Desperation

AT FIFTY-ONE, I'M still racing the bike. Yep. Two-plus decades after I went zooming around the Colorado campus to clinch the 1988 Coors Classic, I still compete in an event called the Town Bike Criterium.

The TBC takes place a couple of miles north of the Colorado campus. Its fields are considerably smaller than the races I formerly contested. In fact, they consist, most mornings, of one rider. And the course varies from day to day, depending on how I'm feeling as I roll out of the driveway.

It is nothing less than a blessing to live in Boulder. But the same cycling culture that makes this community a mecca for road riders can turn into a tyrant, if you let it. If you're not careful you can lose your balance and come to believe that it's not really a workout — not really a *ride* — if you aren't in the saddle for at least, say, two hours. These days, a two-plus-hour road ride — a workout that I once regarded as a mellow recovery spin — now poaches me for the rest of the day. It's not sad. It's just where I am with PD.

To battle the Tyranny of the Big Ride, I started going on these fun little excursions around the neighborhood. I don't bring water — not gonna be out that long. No need for cleated shoes — I'm on my badass Trek District, a belt-driven single-speed designed for commuting and running errands. The unwritten rules of the TBC prohibit Lycra and form-fitted clothing of any kind.

I didn't take a ride, the morning I invented the Town Bike Criterium, so much as the ride took me. I didn't know exactly why I was doing it, until it occurred to me that I was having fun — which was the whole purpose of riding a bike, until I started *racing* a bike.

For a typical TBC, I'll spin up Fourth Street, bang a right on Linden, then a quick left into a neighborhood called Wonderland Hills, and it's game on. Cranking the speed into the low twenties, I'll launch myself into the first cul-de-sac I see, zipping around the circle like a ball on a roulette wheel, swooping back out onto the main drag (after looking both ways, of course). I then repeat that process, through ten or so culs-de-sac, until I've worked my counterclockwise way back to Linden Avenue, then home. I'm so intent on accelerating down the straights, leaning hard into the swooping turns — so busy grinning and making sure I don't get T-boned by some motorist on his way to work — I forget I'm getting exercise.

I get back, and I've elevated my heart rate, opened my lungs, and worked up a sweat, while smiling at untold numbers of neighbors, baffled pedestrians, and confused dog-walkers.

I'm not even a shadow of the sprinter formerly known as Thor. But when it comes to banking those sublime moments, then reflecting on them, using them to get through the day, I'm still the Cash Register.

I have gone, in a sense, from being the fastest cat in the jungle to a kind of squirrel, gathering and storing away small victories. It's not the life I would have chosen. But it's a sweet, full life. A life I embrace.

In the beginning, I was not so accepting. I was lost, bewildered, *pissed*. An incurable disease in this body? No way. And yet, with the same reflexive, impetuous rush that guided me in a bunch sprint, I reached the point after a lengthy journey where I was ready to take action and resolved to afflict my affliction. I would harness my energy, my passion, my anger. I would work to find a cure. In so doing, I told myself, I would save myself, and others.

But first I would need a nudge from an unlikely source, a former Bike Camp client and bike shop owner named Kathy Krumme.

Her father was a charismatic, well-liked businessman in Cincinnati who also happened to suffer from Parkinson's. Kathy was putting together a charity ride to raise funds for Parkinson's research locally at the University of Cincinnati's Neuroscience Institute. She invited me to participate, and asked if she could name the event after me. One thing led to another and she suggested we create a 501c(3) company. More than starting a ride, she and her partner, David Ariosa, created a charitable organization in my name, the Davis Phinney Foundation. And in addition to the ride, she organized a huge gala dinner for the night before, dubbing the entire weekend "the Sunflower Revolution."

When it was my turn to speak, I told the story of my rough ride up the Alpe d'Huez back in 1990. Remember how I almost missed the time cut? I brought the story home by repeating Och's words to me after I crossed the line and collapsed: "Two minutes. You made it by two minutes."

At that, the crowd erupted. But I wasn't finished. "Those two minutes are sort of what I'm facing now," I told the audience. "When you have a neurological disorder with no known cure, you face continuous degeneration. We can find a solution, but we have a time limit. It's going to be tough; it's going to take everything we have to get from the bottom of the Glandon to the top of the Alpe d'Huez before we're out of the race. But we can do it."

I'd just joined this battle against the Body Snatcher. I was all about finding a cure, crossing the line before I missed the time cut. It was a useful metaphor, and it turned out to be a sure-fire applause line.

And you know what? The clock kept ticking. A year went by,

then another year, and another. Still no cure. And it became apparent that I needed to adjust my tactics. I was still a sprinter in the marrow of my bones: this waiting around for good news did not serve me or my fellow Parkinson's peeps. It was too passive.

"By focusing on a cure," I started telling the members of my tribe, "what we're really doing is waiting for somebody to do something for us. We're hiding away, shutting ourselves in. Worse, we're *declining*."

As the DPF grew in size and stature, we also retooled our mission. We could do the most good, I felt, by attacking the despair and surrender and loss of hope that too often attend this disease. By all means we will continue to work for a cure, and to that end we are also aligned with the Michael J. Fox Foundation, which is almost strictly focused on funding research toward finding a cure.

In the meantime, I tell the members of my tribe, *Get out!* Move your body! Meet some friends. Think positively. Focus. Be present for those brief, shining moments. If you happen to be experiencing a bit of tremoring or gyrating, and passersby feel inclined to stare, whose problem is that? Our mission has evolved to help the members of my tribe live well *today*.

To that end, we recently rolled out *Every Victory Counts*, a manual addressing topics ranging from diagnosis to exercise to medications and the effects of your PD on your family and the importance of maintaining a sense of humor in the face of the disease. (The manual can be kept current with downloadable material from www.everyvictorycounts.org.) It is, in short, everything I could have used, but couldn't find, around the time I was diagnosed.

Back in the day, I was in the habit of signing in late, then rolling up to the start line last, with my best game face. Even if I had to fake it a little — if my legs felt heavy or my throat was sore and I sensed a cold coming on — I would still stand there, straddling my bike behind a mask of focused intensity. The other guys in the race didn't need to know I felt like crap. What I wanted them to think when they saw me was, "Uh-oh. Davis is here. I guess we're racing for second." Because a lot of days, no matter how I felt at the start of the race, I was feeling better by the end of it, and they were. Racing for second.

One of the many traits of PD is that it masks your emotions, quite literally by flattening facial responses. I've tried to break out of that by striding to the dais when called upon to speak in front of crowds—with a spring in my step, even if I have to force it. Rather than take the stairs, I'll vault onto the stage. Is the vaulting a shtick? Sure, a little bit. But it's also an act of defiance, a public "in your face" to PD. I want to remind my audience that a lot of the limits in our lives are self-imposed. And I like to remind myself that I've still "got it." It also makes me smile, which immediately wipes the PD mask off my face and, if for only a few moments, makes me feel cured.

That's generally the gist of the speech I'll then deliver. One of the beautiful things about being a bike racer, I tell them, is that when you cross the line first, you get to thrust your arms skyward—a feeling that falls somewhere between sex and found money. Why limit the experience to winning a bike race? And so I prod them into putting down their notebooks and making room to practice . . . winning.

"Now, on the count of three," I will instruct, "everybody . . . arms up!"

I am always inspired by the bedlam that follows: the field of uppercase V's that springs up in the ballroom. A lot of the participants are members of my tribe, so the V's are often wobbling and imperfect. But they are all perfectly defiant. Sometimes we'll do it a second time, just for fun, and because, quite simply, we can.

In 2005, during our third and final year in Marostica, and with my Parkinson's progressing inexorably, I signed on for a two-week stay at the Paracelsus Klinik near St. Gallen, Switzerland. This enlightened institute was founded by Dr. Thomas Rau, a Swiss-born MD who left mainstream medicine because he felt he could do more by incorporating health and wellness principles into a whole-body approach, a philosophy that resonated with me.

I'd heard about Dr. Rau and Paracelsus from Claude Pepin, a fellow member of my tribe, who'd reached out to me earlier. Claude was the first person I'd met who'd undergone deep brain stimulation surgery. It had done wonders for him, dramatically reducing his symptoms. While Claude made a persuasive case, I wasn't ready to commit just then. I mean, it was freaking *brain surgery*.

At Paracelsus I submitted to blood therapies, bodywork, herbal infusions, nutritional therapies, neural injections, and, the most intense experience, an induced fever aimed at stimulating the immune system. Many of my symptoms abated. While my tremor didn't go away, I slept better, felt more relaxed and alive than I had in years. I returned to the clinic several times. But the great feeling I gained from my stays was hard to sustain. As PD exacted an ever-greater toll, I started to rethink my conviction that pharmaceuticals were not for me.

During a brief visit to the States, I had an appointment with Dr. Fredy Revilla, a highly respected neurologist in Cincinnati whom I had met through my work with the DPF. After years of putting it off, of stubbornly walking my own path, I succumbed. I turned, again, to the meds, starting a regimen of Sinemet, and enjoyed near-immediate relief. Why had I waited? Conventional wisdom dictated that Sinemet, while frequently the most effective medicine for managing symptoms, required increasingly higher doses, which, in turn, exacerbated the side effects. It made sense for me, basically, to postpone my Sinemet regimen for as long as possible — which is why I'd stopped using it in the first place.

Dr. Revilla, however, made a persuasive argument as he explained the process to me: the brain protects itself from toxins with a filtering network of blood vessels and cells called the blood-brain barrier. Nutrients can easily reach our brains; toxins have a more difficult time. That's good news for your brain, but bad news if you're trying to feed your brain much-needed, and missing, ingredients — in my case, dopamine. That's the neurotransmitter which, among other things, allows for smooth muscle coordination.

Sinemet contains levodopa, or L-dopa, a dopamine precursor that is able to sneak across the blood-brain barrier. There are drawbacks. One is the on-off cycle. (When the drug is working, you're on; when it's not, you're off.) And if you mistime or overdo your dose, you can become dyskinetic, exhibiting the spastic, involuntary movements often mistaken for PD itself.

The upside, Fredy argued, was that I would be buying time — time to live a fuller, more "normal" existence. Perhaps the drug would work well for only five years, but they'd be years of improved function and dramatically reduced tremor. He pointed out that by the time the Sinemet lost its effectiveness for me, maybe researchers would have come up with some new breakthrough. Connie supported my decision either way, but the truth is, we were both worn down by this battle.

For me the golden age of Sinemet would last only about a year and a half. My response to the drug at first was predictable, and predictably good. And I was *stoked*. I had smooth function, with no tremor, and little dyskinesia. As the side effects worsened, I became a less-than-model patient, trying to outwit the disease by halving a dose here, doubling it there, always seeking the elusive sweet spot that had been so readily available during the golden age.

When my dyskinesia came on, it came on with a vengeance, subjecting me to a whole new level of dis-ease. Finally, I reached a point where the on-off cycle was as bad as taking no meds at all. That point also goes by another name: desperation.

13

Dad, I Gotta Do This

'D RETURNED TO the Tour de France in 2004 almost against my will. In the fourteen years since gutting myself to get through the 1990 Grand Boucle, I hadn't been back, as a rider or spectator. In addition to being a logistical beast — massive crowds, hideous traffic — Le Tour is also an unofficial reunion of guys like me: riders from back in the day. Ex-pros are everywhere, directing teams, doing radio and TV, leading bike tours, and filling VIP tents. I hadn't seen these guys since my diagnosis. They remembered me as a fearsome sprinter. I was returning to them much diminished. Back then, in the summer of '04, I was far more self-conscious of my PD than I am now. The overtness of my symptoms stressed me out — *everyone's looking at me!* — which had the effect of magnifying the symptoms. My old colleagues would strive to keep the pity out of their eyes and expressions, and they would fail. That scene, I knew, would be played out many times, every day, which is why I'd stayed away from the Tour, despite the fact that we lived less than three hundred miles from the French border.

Connie, on the other hand, keenly felt the pull of this grandest of Grand Tours. She longed to witness it, if for no other reason than to fully understand it. As she reminded me, often, she'd never seen the Tour in person.

We'd immersed ourselves in the energy and excitement of the Giro d'Italia, which, by happenstance and pure brilliance, came through Marostica two of the three years we lived there. How about the Tour de France? "Come on," Connie insisted. "Let's go! *Andiamo!*"

I relented, finally, with a huge assist from our friend and Bassano neighbor Tim Maloney, then the editor of Cyclingnews.com. I agreed to write a series of columns from the Tour. In exchange, Tim hooked us up with press credentials, and a blue "media" windshield sticker that was vital to getting around the Tour, allowing us to drive on the actual course, park close to the finish, and generally get behind the ropes. Tim also hustled up passes for Taylor and Kelsey, which is how we ended up with pictures of our ten-year-old daughter hugging one of Lance Armstrong's stuffed lions, the prize given daily to the leader of the race.

I've described the Tour as a terrible beauty, and our experience at the '04 Tour was both beautiful and terrible.

I'd agreed to lend my name, and expertise, to an acquaintance who had started a new tour group, with some of the proceeds going to the fledgling Davis Phinney Foundation. It was a huge undertaking with more than fifty paying clients, run by well-intentioned people who turned out to be completely out of their depth. They started late, missed stages, lost track of clients. The coup de grâce: while descending a mountain road on Bastille Day, the guy in charge of the group broke his hip when he flipped on his bike after running over a client who'd fallen directly in front of him.

With the tour group descending into anarchy, Connie offered to help. On the day of Stage 10, she was pacing a lagging client back to the main group after making a wrong turn, when a cement truck came careening up from behind. Carrying way too much speed into a roundabout, the truck went up on two wheels, then *tipped over*. From his vantage in the follow vehicle behind the accident, Taylor thought the truck had landed on his mother, who for her part feared that it had crushed the rider behind her. In the end, no one was injured — not even the driver of the truck. But it left us deeply shaken — almost as shaken as we would be on what Connie refers to as "the day I fell for George."

It was a Tour rest day. After being waved past security at the US Postal Service team hotel, we were ushered into a room with Lance and his then girlfriend, the singer Sheryl Crow, who immediately befriended Kelsey. I caught up with Lance while Connie walked over to greet an old friend, the cyclist George Hincapie, who was sitting with the rest of the team in the next room. Connie stepped around the end of their long table in the crowded room, failing to notice an opening to a short stairwell in the floor — like a trapdoor minus the door, basically — which was normally cordoned off by a screen. The screen, which had taken to toppling over, had been removed, we were later told. As Connie approached George, she literally disappeared, cartwheeling headlong down the darkened stairwell. In truth, it was a terrifying moment: she could have been seriously injured, or worse. As it was, she emerged traumatized and embarrassed, looking like she'd been in a bar fight. Connie suffered bruises, a mild concussion, and a primo black eye. Kelsey remembers it this way: "Sheryl and I were just starting to have an interesting conversation, then Mom fell into the basement."

The next year was better. We brought our Bike Camp clients to the French ski resort of Courchevel, site of the Stage 10 mountaintop finish, and let the Tour come to us.

Our hotel was halfway up the climb. It was fascinating, in the days before the arrival of the traveling carnival that is Le Tour, to feel the momentum build: the arrival of tourists and campers from all over Europe — all over the world: a trickle at first, then a steady stream, then a flood as the spectacle approached. In the long-standing tradition of Tour fans, we painted the roads, Taylor using a roller and a vast quantity of white latex to leave the message:

LANCE IS MY HERO. In somewhat smaller letters, he spelled out the URL davisphinneyfoundation.org.

And the big day arrived, with first the publicity caravan making its halting way up through town, a convoy straight out of the fevered imagination of Lewis Carroll: a gigantic cup and saucer, followed by a fifteen-foot teapot, which gives way to a varied assortment of floats, enormous sausages and cheese wheels and the like, each advertising a product, each bearing attractive, tanned young people tossing free gifts to the crowd — polka dot caps and gratis issues of *L'Équipe* and Haribo gummi bears.

Next came the squadrons of Tour vehicles: officials, press, VIPs, team support personnel, and more gendarmes than a *Pink Panther* movie. Finally, the riders went by — their pace breathtaking, Armstrong leading an elite selection of riders, his archrival Jan Ullrich laboring and losing ground. The rest of the field rolled through in bits and pieces, and before we knew it, the *spettàcolo* — "the show," in Italian — was over. Until the following day.

Connie headed back to Italy with our Bike Camp clients. T and I followed the Tour. I'd gotten over my initial reservations. The truth was, I felt embraced, not judged, by my old friends and colleagues and rivals. Plus, Taylor and I were getting in quality father-son bonding time, in addition to a fair amount of time-in-the-saddle time, as well.

On the mornings of mountain stages, we'd get on the course a few hours before the peloton came through, soaking up the Tour vibe, smiling at spectators along the road and at our fellow cyclotourists. Having recently resumed taking Sinemet, I found cycling easier, though some days were better than others. When I faltered, Taylor would reach out to push me — just as my old 7-Eleven teammate Sean Yates once did if I was fading on a Tour climb back in the day.

Sometimes I accepted Taylor's help. Sometimes we rode at my more conversational pace. And sometimes I told him to forget about me and just attack the climb, because even then, it took my breath away to see this adolescent, this future world champion, sprint away and power up the mountain. Even then, it was a gift to watch him ride.

We hooked up with Alex Stieda's tour group in Lourdes and rode with them as ride leader guides for a few days. One morning we rode the Col d'Aubisque with a strong group, mostly from the States. T was antsy, feeling his oats, so I told him to go for it, told him I'd see him at the top. Inside a minute he was around the bend and out of sight.

Remember Tony Pranses, of Lima, Ohio? He was the cycling aficionado who, back in the early 1950s, turned my dad on to the pleasures of covering long distances by bicycle. To make those rides through the Buckeye State more interesting — and to give themselves goals — Tony applied European place-names to some of the landmarks and geographic features they rode by. His tongue-in-cheek handle for the highway overpass just outside town, typically the last "hill" they'd sprint for on their way back to Lima: the Col d'Aubisque. And that famous name had always stuck in my head from my father's telling of the tale.

The original Col d'Aubisque, the westernmost of the Tour's epic Pyrenean climbs, is difficult enough to be rated *hors catégorie* — beyond category — in the official rating of the various climbs the TDF passes over. It is also beyond beautiful. Long stretches of the thirteen-mile ascent have been hewn and blasted from near-vertical pitches of rock. The vistas are stunning, almost otherworldly.

Best not to drink them in if you're driving. The Aubisque is steep, narrow, and dangerous. It was on this climb in 1951 that Wim van Est — the first Dutchman to wear the *maillot jaune* — slid out on a patch of gravel and left the road, tumbling sixty feet, coming to rest on a precipice overlooking a vertical drop of more than two thousand feet. Van Est's manager threw him a rope, but it was too short. The manager then tied together some forty spare tires, attached them to the rope, and pulled his rider to safety. The Dutchman lost his yellow jersey that day, but lived to tell the tale.

Like the Aubisque itself, life is alternately cruel and beautiful. On the morning of July 17, 1990, thirty-nine years after Dad and Tony's assaults on the imaginary Col and just a few years after his cancer diagnosis, my father rose early. He was happy, excited, a bit apprehensive. That morning, he would ride the real Col d'Aubisque for the first time.

His cancer had been in remission for three years. Even after the profound attitude adjustment the disease had imposed on him, Dad remained a penny-pinching Yankee. But between his passion for riding his bicycle up mountains, and my mother's desire to get out and see the world, he allowed himself to be talked into signing up for a European bike tour. In 1990, the first of what turned out to be many trips with Breaking Away Bicycle Tours, they chose to shadow the Tour de France as it traversed the Pyrenees. My parents had never seen me ride the Tour before. But on July 17, we had a date at the top of the Aubisque.

I wasn't having a lot of fun during that year's Tour, you may recall. After barely making the time cut on the Alpe d'Huez, I'd continued to struggle, and was more than two hours off the lead. But I was damned if I wasn't going to finish now. Especially with my folks having come this far to catch a glimpse of me. Not surprisingly, I was dropped on the early slopes of the Aubisque. Knowing my parents were stationed at the summit, I dug *deep*, fought my way to the main group just before the summit, then had the temerity to roll to the front of the pack as we crested the climb, giving Damon and Thea a nonchalant smile and wave as I rolled by. I have many memories from my career, but that snapshot on the Aubisque—the pride in my father's Klaxon voice as he bellowed out, "Way to go, Dave! Way to go!"—stands out as one of the most gratifying moments from my racing life. We spend our lives trying to make our parents proud of us. In that moment, my dad could not have been more proud.

Fifteen years later, on the same mountain, with my fifteen-year-old son champing at the bit, I'd encouraged him to go ahead. And there he was, waiting, when I finished the climb, some twenty-five minutes after him. At the sight of his father he channeled his late grandfather, welcoming me to the summit with a broad smile and the words, "Way to go, Dad. Way to go."

From the beginning, Taylor was a stylish rider with a smooth, fluid pedal stroke. He had this effortless panache on the bike. The *tifosi* lining the road, cycling fans from all over Europe, were particularly generous in their shouts of encouragement to the younger cyclists riding the course ahead of the pros. Decked out in a replica of the white jersey signifying the best young rider, purchased at a kiosk, Taylor got a lot of applause, and liked the sound of it—which made him ride that much faster.

On one especially hot day, he rolled up to one of the Aquarel trucks, where workers handed out bottled water to parched spectators. He quickly found himself face to face with a vision: the Aquarel Girl, a sun-kissed, almond-eyed brunette who bestowed upon him a bottle of water and a dazzling smile. They had a "moment"—in his view, at least—then she was gone. Taylor remounted his bike and floated up the rest of the climb. "Wow," he told me later. "I need to spend a lot more time in this country."

He was growing up, becoming a man, starting to think about who he wanted to be. On the Tour rest day in Pau, six days after Lance had taken the yellow jersey in Courchevel, we once again dropped by his team's hotel to say hello. He was more than accommodating—smiling, relaxed, posing for photos, with T's arm slung over his shoulder. That backstage-pass moment stuck with Taylor, who was in an impressionable, searching phase. He was processing information, on the cusp of a fateful decision.

The next morning, we dropped by the "start village," which is assembled near the *depart*, or start, of every stage. Access is tightly controlled; only riders, media, and various Tour bigwigs are allowed in. Roughly the size of a football field, the village is an oasis of amenities and amusements: a magician, some stilt-walkers, computer terminals for those starved of e-mail access. There's also an actual, open-air hair salon, where riders are free to drop in for a trim. Throughout the space, they have these mini-cafés, courtesy of the Tour's title sponsors, where you can peruse a paper over coffee and a croissant. Local chefs serve regional fare: cheeses, breads, sausages, and, *bien sûr,* a sampling of wines. Perhaps most important: there are several kiosks where caffeine vixens in tight shirts and short shorts dispense shots of Grand' Mère coffee. I think Taylor drank more espresso that week than at any other period in his life.

It was in the Tour village, following the rest day, that I introduced Taylor to Axel Merckx, an Olympic medalist and strong all-around rider for the Davitamon-Lotto team. Even though he was fourteen hundred miles into the Tour, with the start of Stage 16 just twenty minutes away, Axel stepped forward and, at six feet three one of the tallest guys in the peloton, stood eye to eye with T. He shook Taylor's hand and they talked for ten minutes. As the son of the great Eddy Merckx, a five-time Tour de France winner whom many consider the greatest rider ever, Axel knew a little bit about the weight of a family name. He and Taylor bonded immediately. He asked T what his hobbies were.

"Soccer is my first love."

"Really? I was crazy about soccer. Played till I was fifteen."

"I'm fifteen."

"Then I started racing bikes."

You could see the wheels turning in Taylor's head. *Tall dude, great rider, started racing at fifteen. Hmmmm . . .* A few days later he'd reached a verdict: "Dad, I gotta do this."

14

The Trenches

I DID A FAIR bit of growing up between the 1987 and 1988 seasons, which would serve me later when I was confronted with far more hardship than a simple bike race. Bike racing is, at the end of the day, something you can quit. I can't quit PD. I am stuck with it.

But the breakthrough I had in 1987 with my dad, who decided, at the end of his sixth decade on earth, to stop hiding his light under a bushel, illuminated my path as well. Inspired by Damon's metamorphosis after his cancer diagnosis, I realized that I could evolve as well.

I wouldn't say I was an *asshole* up until that time, even as I would acknowledge that there are people out there who may debate that point. I was intensely competitive and, in the critical moments before, during, and after races, not always solicitous of the feelings of others.

And my marriage was in trouble. After four and a half years, Connie and I had hit a rough patch. While I'd been moving closer to my father, and my teammates, for that matter, I'd been drifting from my wife. To an extent I had not realized, Connie was still grieving, and unmoored by, the unexpected passing of her mother the previous autumn. Having lived with MS for a quarter century, Darcy had been in failing health. Still, it was a shock when she died suddenly of heart failure at the age of fifty-five. She and Connie had been very close. I should have offered more support during that time. But Connie had always been so strong and able, it was not readily apparent to me how deep was the well of her grief. Both of us traveled extensively (at the height of my cycling career I was gone more than two hundred days a year), and rarely in the same direction. The fabric of our lives, once so seamless, had started to unravel. When I left for Europe at the start of the '88 season, Connie asked me not to call her. We would see how things progressed when I returned. In the meantime, she'd decided that communication would not be productive.

It was a period of soul-searching for both of us, but one that served us and ultimately saved us. When I'd asked her to marry me, I actually asked her if she'd grow old with me. Little did either of us know that, in me, the process would be so accelerated. At the time — in 1983 — I thought we'd be young, hip, and cool forever. Growing old was a notion, not a reality. Though Darcy had a chronic disease, and we'd witnessed the degenerative changes in her wrought by MS, Connie and I never thought, "What if that happens to me?" Who does?

My public persona was that of a good guy with a ready smile, ever eager to oblige the media with a sound bite, always sure to deflect credit to teammates. Behind the scenes, however, I could be a demanding, petulant SOB.

When I originally signed with 7-Eleven I became a vocal proponent of wanting to "represent the brand in the best way possible." Which meant winning, naturally. That fit hand-in-glove with my own all-consuming ambition to win more races than anyone on the planet. Don't blame me, I could say, if I had to be a prick on occasion.

The wonder of my father's transformation, and my strained

relationship with Connie, got me thinking. So when the riders and staff assembled for 7-Eleven's 1988 training camp, I brought a genuine smile, and an extra measure of humility. I did a better job treating people as I would have liked to be treated. The results were fairly dramatic. I actually overheard a female staffer say, "Wow—Davis can be a nice guy!" That stung, but felt good at the same time.

What price did I pay for this maturity, this softening in my heart? My marriage got back on track, and I had the best year of my career.

After a heavy snowfall that February, I was back in Boulder not long before I flew to Florida for the weeklong Tour of Americas, walking with Dad to work. We were yakking it up, enjoying each other's company, when we ran into John Wilcockson, the reporter from *VeloNews*. John commented on my unconventional training for the upcoming race. Cyclists, being highly specialized, avoid extraneous walking during the season. After I won the overall title at the Tour of Americas, taking two stage wins in the process, Wilcockson deadpanned, "Walking in the snow—there must be something *to* that."

I continued to ride strongly throughout that season, winning a stage at the Tour de Romandie and having by far my strongest Tour de France. I finished most stages with the main group, rather than the *gruppetto,* and came in second in the points competition to Belgian Eddy Planckaert. I won the overall title of the Coors Classic. But inevitably, there were lowlights, too.

Along with Milan–San Remo, Liège-Bastogne-Liège is one of cycling's five Monuments, the most prestigious one-day races of the season. Contested since 1892, through the Ardennes region of Belgium, it is known as *La Doyenne*—The Oldest. Just shy of 259 kilometers, back-loaded with such painful and unwelcome climbs as the Stockeu, La Redoute, and the Col de Forges, this course was better suited to the stronger climbers among my teammates, like Wookie or Andy Hampsten. But I'd been riding well, and held out hope for a good result at *La Doyenne.*

For such a revered professional event, you would think the race organizers might have reconnoitered the route and noted a serious problem. The pack was barreling down a slight grade, clipping along at sixty kilometers an hour, when we realized, too late, that a stretch of the tarmac was missing. A road crew had left a three-foot-wide, one-foot-deep trench, which riders were being forced to jump, or bunny hop, over, lifting both wheels off the ground. The pack suddenly looked like a pack of bounding antelopes.

Not surprisingly, as Alex Stieda later recalled, "Some riders mistimed their jumps, and stacked it on the other side, and pretty soon you had these huge crashes, great big piles of guys." Which we soon joined.

No one seemed too badly hurt, but a lot of riders trashed their wheels. Our team car was well back in the caravan, which meant that our mechanic, Rich Gilstrap, had a long run to reach us. He arrived on the scene with one set of wheels — a good start. "The problem," Stieda recalled, "was that there were about six of us that needed wheels."

So Rich ran back to the team car and started cannibalizing spare bikes, eventually showing up with enough wheels to go around. For whatever reason, Alex and I were at the end of the line for new wheels. When we finally started chasing, our pace was halfhearted — we'd begun to think our race was over — until team director Mike Neel pulled alongside, urging us, "C'mon, guys! Everyone's going slow up front. You can catch 'em!"

We drafted off the team car, hitting speeds up to eighty kilometers an hour as we tried to recover lost ground. Eventually, having ridden ahead of Alex, I caught up to the main caravan of team cars, hopscotching from car to car until I found myself tantalizingly close — just another hundred meters! — to the peloton. I was back in the game.

At that moment, an attack went off the front. The pack reacted immediately. I was already "on the rivet," but would have to somehow match this acceleration. *F——!* Lowering my head, I dug deeper still. The race motorcycles flanking me were beeping their horns, alerting the team cars ahead that I was coming through.

Or so I thought. As it turned out, they'd been trying to get *my* attention. I looked up just a moment before smashing face first through the back window of a team car parked in the middle of the road. The driver had stopped to change a wheel for a rider, but failed to pull to the right. It was a Renault wagon — ironically, a team car for the squad sponsored by ISO Glass, a tempered, or "safety," glass that is laminated to hold the fragments in place when it shatters, thus helping prevent injuries.

As became evident to anyone who saw me fly through the window, the ISO Glass team car was not, in fact, equipped with ISO Glass in the rear window. The windshield exploded like a Coke bottle dropped from a skyscraper. My gigantic '80s-style Oakley Factory Pilots kept the shards out of my eyes, which saved my sight. The rest of me, however, was not so lucky.

After impact I thudded backward onto the pavement, bleeding all over the road. My face was bathed in crimson: little skin was visible. (I'd also severed a tendon in my left arm.) Teammate Roy Knickman knelt over me, convinced that I was bleeding to death, then took a seat in the team car, too shaken to continue. Renowned cycling photographer Graham Watson still refers to it as one of his worst days on the job — the day he photographed me bleeding all over the pavement and refused to share the worst of the photos.

When the ambulance arrived, the paramedics wrapped my head like a mummy. Mike Neel had to stay with our guys who were still on the road, and so he made an extraordinary request of Alex. Would he mind dropping out of the race and accompany me to the hospital?

I lay strapped to a slim metal gurney in the back of the little microbus ambulance, completely blindfolded and feeling scared, thinking, *What have I done to myself?* But Alex was amazing. He sat with me, still in his racing kit, holding me steady on the narrow, twisting roads. He would say, "Hold on, Dave — hard right turn," then quiz the driver in French: "How much farther? Come on, let's go!" and then start telling me an off-color "Little Johnny" joke — to keep my mind off the fact that my face looked, as he later told me, "like it had gone through a meat grinder."

During that drive, Alex pushed the paramedics to take me to a big-city or university hospital. "It is not possible," they replied. We ended up at a small clinic outside Liège, where I told Alex, through the bandages, "I can't see anything. You've got to be my eyes."

Soon, they wheeled me in for some x-rays. I lay there, immobile, while a giant overhead machine blasting three gazillion nanograms of radiation moved over me slowly, clicking images. Before it arrived at my midsection, Alex intervened, asking for a lead apron, valiantly defending my reproductive viability. There ensued a discussion among the orderlies, who scoffed at my American fear of radiation. One of them finally produced an industrial rubber glove, which they placed over my junk before continuing.

Next, Alex spoke with the surgeon who would sew me back together. The doctor struck Alex as uber-competent, an assurance that gave me peace of mind as I succumbed to the anesthetic. It turns out the surgeon was definitely trained for this type of work. Five hours later, the job was finished. They'd patched my face and left eyelid back together with 150 microstitches, plus another thirty stitches in my left arm, where I'd severed the tendon. (I still can't extend that pinky — a problem should I ever be invited to high tea.)

Thus ended the most frightening day of my cycling career — a day also marked by a great lesson. I'd learned from Alex the meaning of what it is to be a true friend and teammate.

• • •

I spent the next five days in that hospital outside Liège, with my face wrapped like a character in a *Scooby-Doo* episode. I had no books, no TV, no music, and little company. Mike Neel dropped by a couple of times, but he and the team were staying on the other side of Belgium, with races ongoing, so we spoke only briefly.

I put in a call to Connie to let her know what had happened. Her first words to me: "I thought I told you not to phone me."

Against her wishes, I did call, finding her at the Olympic Training Center (OTC) in Colorado Springs. Having grown weary of flying to corporate speaking engagements, playing the role of "Olympic champion," Connie had begun work on her master's in exercise science at CU, and taken on the responsibility of junior women's national cycling coach.

I told her about the crash, but played it down. Way down. *A few stitches. Nothing serious.* I was OK and I would see her in a few weeks, in Washington, DC, for a special dinner benefiting MS, in honor of her mother. We made some strained small talk and said our goodbyes.

Because I minimized the extent of my injuries, Connie didn't feel it necessary to apprise my parents, who were understandably traumatized when a journalist called to ask them if it was true that I'd sliced off my nose, or worse, in a bad crash. When they were finally able to reach Connie, who had no phone in her room at the OTC, they were upset. Why hadn't she told them about the accident? Because, she replied, I'd told her it was no big deal. Both parties agreed: the stress caused to my parents was my fault. And yet, it wasn't the last time I'd underplay the severity of my condition.

With little else to do, I reflected. On life. On marriage. On cycling. I vowed to get past this setback. After dwelling on it for a few more days in that hospital, the question became, not Will I get back in the game? but How soon can I get back on the bike?

Six days after the crash, one day out of the hospital, I cut the cast off my left arm and rode for an hour and a half. The day after that, I stayed out for seven hours. Ten days after my surgery, the stitches still in my face, I entered a road race in Holland, during which I gave parked cars a wider berth than usual. I was actually in a position to contest the sprint until some Dutch rider grabbed my jersey, pulling me back so he could get ahead. Cursing a blue streak in a variety of languages, I followed the asshole to the area beyond the finish line, where he dismounted and started walking toward me, his dukes up. *Uh-oh,* I thought. Dude had about five inches on me. Pointing to my fresh scars, I yelled: "Not in the face!"

I had nothing to worry about. In short order I was ringed by teammates, and the Dutchman decided he might be safer over by his own team car. Bummed as I was to miss out on a chance for a result, it fired me up that my boys had my back. Alex Stieda made the point later: "Every day in the European peloton was a day in the trenches for us. If we'd learned one thing over there, it was that if we were going to have *any* chance at all, we'd have to lean on each other, and trust each other completely."

15

Rocket Launch

F IVE YEARS AND five world championships later, Taylor's decision to get into bike racing may seem inevitable, foreordained. It wasn't. Connie and I told him, straight up, that there would be incredible hardships and pressure. Don't do this for us, we told him. Do it for yourself, because you love it. Or don't do it.

Both of us believed that the surest way to get kids to despise a sport is to force it on them. Connie grew up in Madison, Wisconsin, across the street from a sheet of ice where she learned to go fast, very fast, on skates. She ended up on the US Olympic team at the age of fourteen. I fell hard for road racing in spite of my parents, not because of them. It makes sense, right? We're at our best when the drive to succeed comes from within. There's a difference between scheduled activities our kids are driven to (think minivan) and activities they're driven to do on their own (think passion).

From the time they were tiny, our kids were out skiing, pedaling, whooping it up on the trampoline — *in movement.*

In the late '90s we bought a small second home in tiny Frisco, Colorado, just ninety minutes from Boulder but close to the ski resorts of Keystone, Breckenridge, and Copper Mountain. The house often overflowed with friends and their kids, one of whom dubbed it the Casa Sportiva—the House of Sport.

When there was enough snow, we'd pile it up high, over fifteen feet, to the railing on the deck, and construct a mini ski-jump over the creek in the backyard. Before long, kids would be flying down that ramp—and catching air—on sleds, inner tubes, saucers, cafeteria trays, you name it.

Winter or summer, the kids had access to sports both regulated (soccer, primarily) and unregulated (freeskiing and cycling). T was an absolutely fearless skier, first following me, but eventually leading off-piste, through the trees, in deep powder and through the terrain park. It wasn't long before he was pestering me: "Let's find some cliffs."

Determined to keep up with her brother, Kelsey became a rocket-fast, aggressive skier as well. I still remember the voice of a shocked British matron, emanating from the chairlift above, as Kels dropped into a steep narrow chute at a resort called Madesimo, in the Italian Alps: "My God! Look at that little kiddie!"

We were always up for an adventurous "mission." One night T and I donned headlamps and hiked to the top of nearby Mount Royal, *in the rain,* pretending to be Army Rangers. On other occasions, we'd strapped on snowshoes and lugged inner tubes up a steep circuitous route above Frisco that we dubbed "the luge run." The payoff? A mile-long slide back down.

Taylor was just six years old in 1996 when I had the bright idea to bring him along on a popular weeklong cycling tour called Ride the Rockies. That year's ride would cover 419 miles, and, as the name suggests, took us over a number of mountains, including 10,857-foot Wolf Creek Pass. We did the ride with my father, whose cancer was still in remission. I loved the idea of getting three generations of Phinney boys out on the road together.

We started in Cortez, in the far southwest corner of Colorado, with T and me on the tandem, Dad on his beloved Serotta Ti. (I'd rigged the tandem with a high-mounted bottom bracket—so T's legs could reach the pedals.) The plan was to keep it low-key, keep it fun. Taylor would ride as far with me as he liked on a given day, then jump in the car with his grandma, at which point I would swap the tandem for a single bike, then cruise to the finish with Damon.

It doesn't take much for me to poach myself these days. But in the summer of '96, four years before my diagnosis, I still had plenty of the old power. Taylor and I were cruising past people at twenty-five miles an hour—even when he kicked back and put his feet on the handlebars, as he did every so often.

I know he had *some* fun. We stayed in hotels. Every evening, we joined my mom and dad and our fellow cyclo-tourists taking in the local scene. Best example was participating in the Native American dances in Pagosa Springs that were part of this unique, cool event. We damn near gave Dad a coronary, blowing by him at fifty-plus miles per hour on the way down Wolf Creek Pass. Looking back on it, that probably wasn't such a hot idea. But the kid was already *skiing* at 40 mph. As we rocketed down Wolf Creek, I kept asking him, "You OK, T?" And he'd shout back, "This is AWESOME!"

Taylor averaged twenty-five or thirty miles a day on the bike with me. At some point, he would make the following observation:

"I think Grandma's probably getting pretty lonely in the car . . ."

As the ride went on, his concern for his grandmother cropped up earlier and earlier in the day.

A couple of months later—by this time he was seven—Taylor asked me out of the blue, at dinner one night, "Dad, are we gonna do that Ride of the Rockies next year?"

I very much wanted to, I told him, but I had a scheduling conflict.

I was surprised to see his relief, and more surprised when he reported, "Well, that's good. Because I don't think I'm going to ride my bike at all next year." And true to his word, he took the year off. OK. Point taken. Lesson learned. Too much is too much. I'm glad T called me on it.

Taylor enjoyed our Bike Camps not because he had a chance to ride with the groups (a rarity), but because by the time he was ten, we'd dubbed him our "Corner King." We'd set up a series of cones to teach our clients how to take corners with control and assurance. At an early age, he'd mastered the skill of arcing tight turns at speed. He used to blow the grownups away with his ability to zip around those cones without sliding out. Those skills serve him well to this day.

The night missions, the cycling, the snowshoeing and activity-intensive weekends at Casa Sportiva weren't overtly designed to steer kids toward careers in endurance sports. I'm not that calculating. They were just . . . fun. And if they were developing skills that serve them to this day, if they were cultivating a lifelong love of the outdoors, well, so much the better. I was having fun, too, and giving them something that I didn't get enough of when I was growing up.

My greatest fear, once I found out what I was carrying around, was that the PD would prevent me from raising Kelsey and Taylor the way I wanted to raise them; that it would force me to spend the rest of my days quaking ineffectually on the sidelines of their lives, or absent from them altogether. While this disease gets in the way, every day of my life, that has simply not been the case. Ask Taylor if he thinks I've been absent from his life. I'm a man from whom much was taken but to whom more has been given.

When I was diagnosed, both my children instinctively followed their mother's example: they understood early on that because of this illness, they would need to be more patient and considerate than if I was well. They would have to sacrifice, for me. Parkinson's is tough, but it's forced us to come together, to be stronger. Taylor is twenty as of this writing; Kelsey, sixteen. I'm exceptionally close to them now, because we've been close all along. Taylor grew up listening to me, sharing with me, confiding in me. We never lost that. While it didn't surprise me, it did warm my heart to read his remarks, made to a magazine writer in the spring of '09:

> My father was so much younger than the other Dads his age, if you know what I mean. There's a lot of stuff he can't do now, but we've already done so many cool things together.
>
> The truth is, he put so much time into raising me, I feel like I have this huge debt. I've got a lot to give back to my Dad, and I try to do that by winning bike races.

As I've mentioned, the Davis Phinney Foundation was born at the 2004 Sunflower Revolution, a weekend-long event that included a one-hundred-kilometer charity ride. The ride isn't supposed to be competitive, but it always ends up being *fast*. For the first few years, my old friend Wayne Stetina would hammer up front till there were just a few riders left, and then there would be a sprint to the finish among the lead group.

Late in the summer of '05, following our move back to the States from Italy, that elite bunch included Taylor. Despite having just turned fifteen, he followed wheels and took his turns at the front like a pro. When the endgame arrived, T surprised everyone by exploding out of the group and crossing the line first. Of course he *had* to thrust his arms up, mimicking my old victory salute, which was a problem, considering that the road took a sharp right turn twenty meters past the finish. T looked great — right up to the moment he locked his brakes and skidded into the barricades, his rear wheel pitching up like the back end of a bucking bronco.

"Hey, at least I won," he pointed out to those who needled him for that typically Phinneyesque flourish.

That same week, Wayne sent an e-mail to Jonathan Vaughters,

director of the Colorado-based Slipstream-Chipotle cycling team. The gist of his note: You're an idiot if you don't sign this kid.

Among JV's bright young stars was Wayne's nephew, Peter, who was three years older than Taylor and who'd won the road race at that year's US junior national championships. Taylor was already on JV's radar, despite the fact that he had yet to race a single sanctioned event. On Wayne's recommendation, Vaughters signed him.

Beneath the professional ranks, road racing branches out into various age groups. For riders older than eighteen, called seniors, there are categories for competitors of different ability, ranging from newbie Category 5s to the uber-fit, tactically savvy almost-pros of Cat 1. Taylor started out with a handful of local junior and Cat 4 races but quickly graduated to Senior Cat 3, where he stayed for the remainder of that season. We found ourselves staking out viewing spots on the side of the road, settling into the same camping chairs we'd toted along to soccer games.

His learning curve was steep. He attacked out of the gate on his first-ever race, a tactic that had worked well against the juniors, but which blew up in his face one morning, on a modified version of the Morgul-Bismark loop, a notorious section of the late Coors Classic. The older guys laughed and let him go. Sure enough, T got caught, then dropped. But he fought back, demonstrating a mental toughness, a resolve that he was going to need if he intended to stick with this sport. During one race he came chugging along, dropped by the main bunch. Thrusting a PowerBar at him, Connie shouted, "Just EAT!" He did, came back to life, caught the lead pack, and got a top-ten finish.

Beneath that easygoing, sometimes-goofball exterior blazed a roaring fire. He was in contention for a victory at the US junior criterium nationals, but he crashed on the last lap. He was so pissed that he threw his bike over the barriers, reminding me of the time a then-nineteen-year-old Greg LeMond had done the same thing at a race in France. While I didn't exactly approve of Taylor's tantrum, I understood it. What I did applaud, what I could relate to, was how much he cared about the result, how badly he wanted to win.

In August of 2007, Taylor's second season as a bike racer, we flew to Aguascalientes, Mexico, more than a mile above sea level in the mountains northwest of Guadalajara, for the junior world championships. Taylor was entered in the individual time trial, a race against the clock. He'd just turned seventeen and would be going up against eighteen-year-olds. This being his first international competition, we had no idea what to expect. A top ten would've thrilled us.

Riders in a time trial go off at one-minute intervals. There were only a handful of guys left to start behind him when Taylor rolled down the ramp for two laps of the fourteen-kilometer course. Riding shotgun in the follow car, I got the distinct impression that T was smoking the course—a hunch confirmed by his first-lap split, which put him slightly ahead of everyone.

"Taylor, you're on best time!" I shouted out the window, my voice cracking. He found an extra gear on the second lap, catching and passing several of the riders in front of him, whipping through the final roundabout with such velocity that we, in the car, lost sight of him. He was riding so fast, so powerfully, that I was reduced to a state of shocked incredulity, as is evident on a YouTube video shot from the back seat by his teammate Ben King, in which I exclaim, "Holy f——g s—t! Taylor's gonna be world champion!"

When I finally caught up to him, Taylor was seated behind a barricade, keeping a lid on his emotions until the last few riders came through. Even after it became official—the kid was the junior world champ!—he worked hard to exude a studied cool, which was made far more difficult by the sudden, dramatic arrival of Connie, who'd run roughly a mile to the finish and who proceeded to smother him in a long, maternal hug.

As the navy-blazered UCI official slipped the world champion's rainbow jersey over Taylor's head; as Taylor used American Sign Language to say "I love you" to the crowd; as he politely accepted a bouquet from a local girl in traditional folk dress; as the national anthem played, it dawned on us that we were witnessing a debut of sorts, a coming out. The Start of Something Big. As Connie predicted not long after, "His life will never be the same" — which meant, by extension, that our lives would never be the same. And, as usual, she was right.

In two years he'd gone from raw neophyte to junior world champion. So, what next? Back in Aguascalientes, he'd gone to watch an evening of track cycling at the velodrome. His curiosity was piqued.

The velodrome is a banked, oval track used for a variety of fixed-gear races, all of which fall into two broad categories: sprint and endurance. We had an inkling Taylor might excel in the individual pursuit, a four-kilometer race contested by two riders, who start on opposite sides of the track and "pursue" each other. He was so smooth on the bike, so efficient and still from the waist up — every milliwatt of energy going into the pedals — that it seemed he'd be a natural in the pursuit, as his mother had been. A quarter-century earlier, Connie had won the world championship in this event.

A few weeks after the junior worlds, we flew to Southern California. After a morning of boogie boarding with his buddy, a younger junior named Robin Eckmann, Taylor went with Connie to the velodrome in Carson, California. Roger Young was expecting him.

An old friend, former teammate of mine, and legendary cycling coach, Roger is also the manager of that velodrome. Connie had called ahead to let him know that we might have a pursuiter on our hands. Drop by "any time," came the reply, and so it began.

Roger put Taylor on one of the Felt training bikes he keeps on hand for beginners, and told him to have fun. Rather than be intimidated by the forty-five-degree banked oval, Taylor ate it up, which should not have surprised us. He loved throwing spins and tricks on his twin-tip skis in the half-pipe at Copper Mountain. He was very much at home on banked surfaces. He took to the track immediately, demonstrating both top-end speed and an innate sense of pace. By the end of his second day, "on a borrowed bike in the wrong gear," Roger recalled, T rode a pursuit time that basically would have qualified him for the US national team. Roger looked at Connie and said, "I think we have our next national champion."

"You don't have to teach a cheetah to be a cheetah," Roger would later tell reporters, "and you don't have to tell this kid how to go fast on a bike."

The next race on the calendar was the US elite national track championships, to be held at the velodrome in Carson. Sitting beside Taylor on the flight to LA was Slipstream coach Allen Lim, an articulate, funny, and superbright individual with a PhD in exercise physiology.

After playing a psychology game with Taylor during the flight, Allen told us that our son's worldview was "infinitely upbeat and optimistic."

Overly optimistic, some would say. Considering that he'd never raced on the track before, it seemed a bit of a stretch to enter him in the elite national *track* championships.

It seemed a stretch, that is, to everyone but Taylor. He wanted to go for it. Working through our contacts at USA Cycling, we finagled an entry for him, which didn't go over so well with some of the older "trackies." (Others, like former national champions Brad Huff and Mike Friedman, could not have been more patient and encouraging.) How had this newbie with zero racing experience wormed his way in? Those questions went away after T won the event. Quite comfortably.

Back at that junior nationals weekend where Taylor had lost the race but won the unofficial award for Longest Bike Toss, I'd chatted with Sean Petty, the chief operating officer at USA Cycling. Taking note of T's fluid pedal stroke and general smoothness on the bike, we'd agreed he might have a future in pursuiting. "Who knows," Sean declaimed, "the kid could end up in the next Olympics!"

We laughed, and clinked beer glasses to the prospect, unlikely as it was.

A few months later, Taylor had a decision to make. The individual pursuit was an Olympic event; the Beijing Summer Games ten months away. The Union Cycliste Internationale (UCI) had decreed that riders must be eighteen to compete in the games; Taylor's eighteenth birthday arrived six weeks before the opening ceremony.

Only sixteen spots were available, and they were earned through World Cup events, world rankings, and the world championships. Unfortunately, the international track season was already half over, and the major players in the world rankings had already earned points. With zero ranking points, Taylor was already, umm, in the hole. Over the dinner table we laid out the qualifying criteria, the lap times of Bradley Wiggins, the defending Olympic champion and a past world champion, and speculated on what was possible. It seemed like Mission: Impossible.

In addition to entering five World Cup events on four different continents, there was the small matter of arranging for him to miss most of his senior year of school at Boulder High. (Fortunately, he had plenty of credits to skate through his final two semesters. And we got fantastic support from the school, and his counselor, Claire Sanford, a Boulder High classmate of mine.) Another hurdle was *dinero:* USA Cycling wasn't able to contribute much to the equation. JV agreed to send the Slipstream guys to the first World Cup in Sydney, and USAC picked up part of the tab for the rest of the races. Then — and this was huge — a private sponsor stepped up with a generous donation to help bridge the gap.

We laid it out for Taylor. Theoretically, he could qualify for the Olympics. But his times would have to come down. Considerably. There was a strong chance that the whole thing could end up being a colossal misadventure. If he wanted to go for it, we told him, we would support him. Connie would even fly around the world with him.

Taylor went to bed and slept on it. In the morning I went to his room and asked what he was thinking. It seemed like a daunting task, he admitted. It might be a big mistake. "But I don't want to look back on this and say I didn't at least try. Let's do it."

It is the natural, irrevocable cycle of life: in youth we rise, with age we wither and decline. But the process is supposed to be *gradual*, for crissakes. In my own household this universal dynamic was playing out at warp speed. T was coming up like a brilliant sunrise, and I was . . . I was not doing so well. My trajectory, slightly downward since our return from Europe, had become markedly steeper over the previous six months or so. My relationship with Sinemet, the "gold standard" med for Parkinson's, once so harmonious, grew increasingly contentious throughout 2007. I was popping more pills and suffering worse side effects. I was finding it increasingly harder, and sometimes impossible, to judge exactly when that window of good function would open, and how long it would stay open.

Having weighed the option for several years, I'd finally signed on for deep brain stimulation surgery. My desire for relief outweighed, in the end, my fears about doctors boring holes in my skull and poking around in my gray matter. The man who did most to allay those fears was my friend Dr. Jaimie Henderson, director of the Stanford program in Stereotactic and Functional Neurosurgery, who would be performing the procedure. My good response to Sinemet, Jaimie informed me, indicated a high probability that the DBS would succeed. The operation was originally scheduled for December 2007. Taylor having undertaken his Olympic quest, I postponed till the following spring.

Meanwhile, my son and I proceeded in opposite directions: he was gaining speed and strength, seemingly by the day; I was tremoring harder than ever. Even as the Body Snatcher dragged me to an ever-lower place, I was blessed with this balm, this windfall: Connie and I had bequeathed to the cycling world a talent that, it seemed, would quickly surpass our own.

I was in no condition to follow him to the four corners of the earth as he set out to earn his spot on the Olympic team. But I was grateful that Connie would be with him. Those two (sometimes joined by Kelsey) would fly more than one hundred thousand miles, from Australia to China to Denmark to England to Italy to South Africa to France to England to Beijing and home. (Plus numerous trips to LA for training.) In addition to mom, Connie's hats included chef, chaperone, travel agent, problem solver, and, "on a few slow days," riding partner. Their first stop:

— Sydney. In his third-ever competitive pursuit, in a borrowed skin suit (thanks, Brad Huff!), on a borrowed track bike (much obliged, Magnus Backstedt!), Taylor came out smoking on that velodrome, featured in the 2000 Olympics. He had the fastest time to the halfway, then faded to ninth. He showed raw speed, but failed to properly pace himself. Still, his 4:28 did pull down two precious World Cup points, in addition to lopping nearly seven seconds off his previous best time (granted, he'd only ever ridden two previous pursuits). Still, I cringed watching the videotape. After borrowing that bike from Magnus, Taylor hadn't properly dialed in his position, making for an uncomfortable, inefficient ride. After that race, using Skype and pictures taken on T's iPhone, I did my best to correct his bike-fit from afar. It wasn't perfect, but T felt better on the bike as a result, and his training times improved. Second stop:

— Beijing. Connie, Kelsey, and Taylor arrived at midnight, wilting with exhaustion. Connie stressed about the smoggy air, the astounding traffic on Beijing's streets, and the lack of sleep T was getting. (Their heads didn't hit the pillow till 3 A.M.)

While his mother absorbed the fatigue and anxiety, Taylor was smiling and serene. He showed up at the Laoshan Velodrome refreshed, chipper, ready to scorch the track. He was paired with the German Robert Bartko, the 2000 Olympic champion at this distance. We worried about the effect on Taylor's psyche if Bartko caught him.

We should've been worried about Bartko's feelings. T got off to another sizzling start, held his speed, and dropped another four seconds off his personal best, demolishing the German by six seconds and just making it into the final four—the medal round (the top four times from qualifying advance, with the fastest two times racing off for gold and silver, while the next two fastest race for the bronze).

It was the middle of the night in Boulder when Taylor's race for third place began. Kelsey dialed me up on Skype—I couldn't sleep anyway—then trained the lens of the MacBook on the track. Going up against Alexander Serov, Taylor took his customary early lead, only to watch the savvy Russian pull ahead by a full second halfway through the race. Slowly, agonizingly, T started closing on Serov. With seven laps to go the gap was down to 0.7. With three laps to go, T was within 0.3. On the bell lap it was anyone's race. I was shouting in an empty house as Kelsey pointed the lens at the scoreboard: Taylor had lost by a tenth of a second.

So shines a good deed in a weary world: Despite his disappointment, Taylor made the rounds of the infield, seeking out each of the three riders who'd beaten him, introducing himself, congratulating them, a gesture that impressed his parents as much as anything he did on the bike that day.

After spending Christmas in Frisco, Colorado, at the Casa Sportiva, Team Taylor (now including me!) ventured west, to his next World Cup event, this one closer to home in . . .

—Carson, California, on the outskirts of LA. It felt good to be back on his turf, the track where he'd first learned this discipline, all those years ago. Actually, it had only been four months. But it felt like longer. Of note: he'd returned Backstedt's backup bike and was now running a sleek, fast, custom TK1 Felt track bike.

By this time, mid-January of '08, my symptoms were unrelenting. The pills I took on the day of Taylor's race wore off faster than usual, leaving me in full-on shake-and-bake mode in the moments before he took to the track. Where I was nervous for him, he was calm, focused, unflappable as he warmed up on his rollers. The robust midday crowd included a sizable contingent of reporters, most of whom were there to see the rising star known then as Mini-Phinney.

The time came for him to remove his iPod earbuds, don his teardrop-shaped aero helmet, and head over to the start line. Problem: a well-intentioned teammate had trimmed the straps on his helmet, to reduce drag. Now the opposing ends of the buckle wouldn't attach under his chin.

Solution: a plastic zip tie. Once the helmet was firmly on, I attempted to trim the end of the zip tie, but my hands were shaking. It didn't go well.

"Dad," said Taylor after I fumbled for a few moments, "give me the scissors. You're gonna kill me." He smiled, and I marveled at his calm. Ten minutes later he was cooling down after routing his pair, Ireland's David O'Loughlin, by more than five seconds.

Focusing on not going out too fast in that night's final, he fell half a second behind Dutch rider Jenning Huizenga. No matter. With an amped-up crowd beating on the boards, Taylor's final kilo was his fastest, his margin of victory a fat two seconds. Coming off the track, he was embraced, in turn, by an extremely hoarse Roger Young, beaming national endurance coach Andy Sparks, Slipstream coach Allen Lim, and Taylor's personal coach, Neal Henderson. But no one hugged him longer, or harder, than I did.

Later that night, after the interviews and the doping controls, we found an In-N-Out Burger and shared some news with Taylor. Following his morning ride, the British team had lodged a protest against him, claiming that the angle of his arm, as he rode the bike, was less than the required 120 degrees. (Taylor is six four, outside the limits expressed by the regulations, and somewhat at the mercy of the commissaires, who'd signed off on his position that morning.) To appease the Brit protest, T's mechanic made a modest, half-centimeter adjustment. No one told Taylor, who didn't notice the tweak during his ride.

Connie wondered aloud what the Brits were about. "Interesting that they'd challenge now," she mused. "If it were poker, I'd say they played their card too soon."

Interrupting his intake of fries, Taylor added this to the conversation: "Hmmm. They must be afraid of me."

We headed back to the hotel for a too-brief night's sleep. Taylor was heading home first thing. Next stop:

— Boulder High's Winter Ball, with his then-girlfriend, a six-foot state-champion swimmer and model named Sophie Allen. He enjoyed himself so well at the dance, and during the all-nighter that followed, that he came down with a virus, which he then took with him to . . .

— Copenhagen, for the final event of the World Cup season. The capital of Denmark is one of the most attractive, livable cities in all of Europe — which didn't end up meaning much to Connie and Taylor, considering that the velodrome had been built on a bog twenty kilometers outside town. The team stayed nearby, in a sterile, no-frills hotel called Zleep.

In the weeks leading up to this event, "zleep" was all Taylor wanted to do. He had hugely swollen glands, a slight fever, and could barely get off the couch. But he was still going pretty fast in training. He and Connie decided to go for it.

Taylor needed two points to finish first in the World Cup standings — which would lock down an Olympic berth. He got one. The good news was that his time, 4:31, was probably a world record for someone in the throes of mononucleosis — which he had, as we learned when he got home. The bad news was that, although he finished the season tied in points with the Ukrainian rider Volodymyr Dudya, that tie was broken based on number of wins.

After being congratulated by UCI director Gilles Peruzzi — "You've won the World Cup overall title" — Taylor had his bubble burst in a big way. Five minutes later, Monsieur Peruzzi was apologizing to T: "I'm sorry. You did not win."

Back in the States, getting updates on the phone, I felt whipsawed and helpless. He won! He's qualified for the Olympics! He didn't win. He has not qualified for the Olympics. He's in tears. We're coming home.

Cycling is like life: it exalts us, then casts us into the depths. Taylor could grasp that, intellectually. Now, for the first time, he had to live it. T was silent and despondent in the way that only teenagers can be. As he put it then, "I wanted to evaporate into thin air, to simply be somewhere, anywhere, else."

Last stop, for a little while, at least:

—Manchester, England, for the world championships at the end of March. After returning home and seeking the healing powers of, among other specialists, my Boulder-based acupuncturist, Dr. Ming Zhou, Taylor finally got the upper hand on the mono virus he'd been carrying around since January.

On the day of his race at the worlds, he and the rest of the US contingent got a 7 A.M. wake-up call from UCI drug testers, who were out for blood. Literally. Welcome to the big leagues, kid!
After starting cautiously that afternoon—too cautiously—T failed to make the final, having qualified eighth. Yet there was cause for joy. En route to his new personal-best time of 4:22.36, he'd broken the world junior record in the 3k. Oh, and by the way, he'd hung on to his third-place overall in the UCI world rankings. The top five received automatic invites to the Olympics. At the age of seventeen, five months after his first-ever pursuit, Taylor Phinney had qualified for the Olympics. The kid was going to Beijing!

While in Manchester we were interviewed by Nick Watt, the London correspondent for ABC News. Nick was putting together a segment on Taylor. Watching it later, looking at myself, I see a man gyrating, twitching, jumping out of his skin. That extreme dyskinesia was a side effect of the Sinemet pills, which, by that time, I was throwing back like Tic Tacs. By April 2008 my symptoms were up in my face in a way they had never been before. I was very near the end of my rope, and it convinced me that I'd made the right decision on surgery.

Two days after flying home from England, Connie and I got on a plane for San Francisco. We then drove to Palo Alto, and set up camp at the home of Jim and Sheila Ochowicz. The DBS procedure would take place at Stamford, in four phases over the course of several weeks. Phase one: the day after we arrived in California, Dr. Jaimie Henderson shaved my head, then screwed five bolts, or "fiducials," into my skull. I already walked a little like Frankenstein, thanks to the PD; with a couple more of those bolts on either side of my neck, I could've looked like him.

"What if they go in," Connie had joked, "and there's nothing there?" In the anxious days before "go time," Connie expressed concern that, when they drilled the holes, my "stories" might somehow "escape," streaming into the ether, floating above the operating table, gone for good.

Her joking masked a shared concern: What if it doesn't work? What if, in addition to not alleviating the symptoms of my Parkinson's disease, the operation altered my brain chemistry, changing me in some profound way? What if it made me worse?

With his calm, confident demeanor, Dr. Henderson eased our concerns. Based on my age and disease progression, Jaimie reassured me, there was a high probability of improvement in my symptoms.

Those five fiducials served as markers for the next important step in the DBS procedure. Using advanced computer programs that melded CAT scans and MRI images, Jaimie was soon working with a 3-D image of my brain. Equipped with that "map," he knew precisely where to place the electrodes for brain stimulation. The target: an area called the subthalamic nucleus (STN), located adjacent to the substantia nigra, a kidney-bean-sized part of the brain, one on each side of the central cortex, responsible for the production of dopamine. It's the part of the brain that, for reasons not yet known, is selectively destroyed by Parkinson's.

Before we start shaking, people with Parkinson's exhibit other symptoms — vague clues that we only recognize as symptoms in hindsight. As I described earlier, I used to notice a kind of numbness, or *heaviness* in my left leg. My left foot would cramp and seize up, especially after hard races. And I was dog-tired all the time. Finally, I couldn't control the tremor in my left hand.

It was that undeniable, slap-in-the-face symptom that forced me, finally, to see a doctor. Ten years later, I found myself stretched out on an operating table, marshaling my courage as the drill bit into my skull. Phase two — the surgery proper — had begun. Because the doctors needed my feedback during the four-and-a-half-hour operation, the anesthesiologist didn't put me all the way under. It had also been necessary for me to go off my Parkinson's meds twenty-four hours before the procedure. By the time the surgery rolled around, my body was in open rebellion: tremoring, spasming, cramping. While my skull was anchored by a kind of high-tech manacle, the rest of me thrashed like a flounder on the deck of a Boston Whaler.

While I lay on that table, wondering how the hell I was going to get through the hours that followed, the thought came to me: *Who better than I to endure this torture?* For eighteen years, suffering for hours at a time was what I'd done for a living. And so, as I underwent brain surgery, I consciously disassociated, allowing my mind to wander, time-traveling to a long-ago ordeal. If I could ride over a mountain, in a blizzard, on an afternoon that went down in the annals of cycling as one of the most miserable days in the history of the sport, I could get through this. Stage 16 of the 1988 Giro d'Italia was my most epic day, ever, on a bicycle.

16

The Gavia

BY THE SPRING of 1988 it had been nearly three decades since the Giro d'Italia ventured over the Passo Gavia. It had been out of circulation for so long that many Italian riders, and their directors, failed to grasp how hard it was. They heard the stories from the old-timers, nodded politely, then filed them away. As former Giro winner Gianni Motta told our 7-Eleven team leader, Andy Hampsten, on the eve of the race, "They think it's just another climb."

We knew it wasn't just another climb. The Passo di Gavia is a narrow, steep, and (at that time) partially unpaved beast lurking in the Italian Alps. It is intimidating in every way: grades pitching up to 18 percent; not a lot of guardrails, but plenty of long, straight stretches ending in switchback turns. Local lore had it that wolves prowled the upper reaches of this mountain, which the Giro hadn't crossed over since 1960. After 1988, it would be in no hurry to get back.

We knew all this ahead of time because we had Max Testa. For seventeen years, his family had rented a ski house in Bormio near the base of the Gavia. He'd been riding it, on bicycle and motor-cycle, since he was a boy. For months, ever since the Giro course had been unveiled, Max had been wearing us out with talk of this obscene climb, this glorified goat track, with its ominous headstones — memorials to loved ones who left the road, and this earth, in that order. He spoke of the back side of the mountain, a perpetually chilled valley seldom penetrated by the sun. Max was warning us to bundle up for the descent side of the Gavia even *before* we got the weather report for June 5, 1988.

It was atrocious.

We awoke that Sunday morning to the sound of rain on the roof of our hotel in Chiesa Valmalenco, down valley from the Gavia. The hotel's elevation was just over three thousand feet; the summit of the Gavia is eighty-six hundred feet. At a meeting that morning, a Giro official told all the team directors that he was in frequent contact with a road crew at the top of the mountain. Normally, this pass would not yet be open. But they'd been plowing drifting snow off the road for weeks in anticipation of the race. It was snowing at the summit, but it was a wet snow on a bare road. Conditions were not icy. It was cold, but not dangerous, he said. Unless you weren't prepared for the cold.

The race was on.

At the direction of Och and Mike Neel, our staff embarked on what amounted to a scavenger hunt, fanning out around the village, buying anything that looked warm: ski gloves, balaclavas, wool hats, winter jackets, and the like. They put the clothes in a pile in the middle of a room. Och instructed each of us to fill a bag with warm clothes. That bag would be handed to us at the summit, so we wouldn't freeze during the twenty-five-kilometer descent, which promised to be more miserable than the climb itself.

Different teams prepare for athletic contests in different ways. Our process was simple; we slathered ourselves up like channel swimmers and then went old school: wool and more wool. The European tradition of bike racing celebrated machismo. If it's cold, dab your legs with liniment, throw on a rain cape, and go. That's how Fausto Coppi did it, how Raymond Poulidor and Jacques Anquetil and Eddy Merckx had done it. That's how cyclists would always do it. Right?

We were not born of that tradition, had not sprung from that mindset — recall the skin suits and the Gore-Tex. Of course we wanted to win, but we weren't averse to mitigating our suffering along the way — especially if it could *help us win*. In addition to having the best pure climber in the race, Andy Hampsten, we were the best-prepared team at the Giro that day, in part because our judgment was unclouded by the "hard man" ethos held sacred by the Euros. We had Och waiting for us atop the climb with warm, dry clothes — and he was the *only* director who did that. It was one thing to be a hard man. It was another to be frozen stiff.

Within ten minutes of the start, everyone in the peloton was soaked with freezing rain. On the brief, innocuous descent of the first climb, the modest Passo dell'Aprica, all of us were shivering uncontrollably. Next came a drag race up the Valtellina Valley, as teams sought to position their climbers for the assault of the Gavia.

As I lay in the OR during my DBS surgery, Andy's recollection of that day came back to me. And it helped. "One of the ways I got my courage up," he confided long after the race, "was by looking my competitors in the face. And everyone was terrified." On the approach to the climb, a few riders spun up alongside us. "Hey Andy," one of them said. "You're not gonna attack today, are you?"

He made no reply. When those guys drifted back, Andy told us to ride faster.

Rain and sleet gave way to snow as we passed through the little town of Ponte di Legno, then turned left over an old wooden bridge. The road kicked up to a 3 or 4 percent grade. The climb had begun. Andy held his fire.

Drawing on his memories of the area, back in the hotel Max had described to us a place where a modern, two-lane road would

sweep to the left, then enter a stand of ancient evergreens. The
road would narrow to a single lane, then turn to dirt. "There will
be a sign that says 'Narrow Road, 16 percent,'" he told us. "That
sign is fourteen kilometers from the summit."

Andy had thrown off his jacket on the way to the climb. Bob
Roll tells the story of being asked by our *capo* to drop back to
the team car to get him another jacket. The pace was near frantic at this point, but Bob dutifully swung to the side, freewheel-
ing along with his hand in the air as the pack flew past. Seeing his
signal, race officials called up Mike Neel in the follow car. Bob finally got the jacket, stuffed it under his jersey, and, with supreme
effort, clawed back all the ground he'd just given away. He reached
Andy just as the grade steepened, only to be told that our leader
had changed his mind. Cussing in seven different languages, Roll
threw the jacket at a *tifoso*. The life of a domestique can be a bitch.

Andy's strategy wasn't complicated. Everyone in the peloton,
everyone in Italy, knew he was going to attack. "My only tactic,"
he related, "was to take the big stick and swing it." When the road
turned to dirt, attack he did. And he was gone.

A breakaway of a dozen riders had bolted earlier. Sailing up the
switchbacks, Andy picked them off, one at a time. By now the rain
had given way to plump snowflakes, as if we were riding through a
just-shaken snow globe. When one of the mechanics handed Andy
a cycling cap through the window, he passed his hand over his
head to squeegee the water out of his hair. At that moment, he remembers, "A big snowball rolled off my head, and down my back."

Eventually Andy was handed a folded, frozen rain jacket near
the summit. The only items he took from Och were a dry hat and a
bottle of hot tea. Looking down at his legs at one point during the
descent, he said he noticed a rime of ice covering his shins. After
that, he stopped looking down. He didn't want to know.

He was beaten to the summit by the Dutchman Johan van der
Velde, the lone survivor from that early breakaway. Europeans

tended to accuse the Americans of "kamikaze" tactics, but it was
Van der Velde's heedless, balls-out assault of the Gavia that struck
some of us as vaguely suicidal. Racing in short sleeves, without
arm warmers or even a hat, he charged through the blizzard as if
it were not happening. The strategy worked brilliantly . . . until he
crested the mountain and started down.

The storm, you see, was coming from the far side of the Gavia,
the north side, which meant that the weather would be worse on
the descent, as Max had assured us and as Johan now discovered.
After careening his way through the first few switchbacks, he began shivering so violently that he retreated to the team car, sipping
hot tea and cognac, for the better part of an hour. Having summited the climb in first place, he lost nearly forty-seven minutes to
the leaders on the descent.

Having helped deliver Andy to the base of the climb, I clicked
into survival mode, grinding my way up the beast with a dwindling *gruppetto*. As the snowstorm blew in heavier, I felt disoriented and isolated, even wondering, at one point, *Is this the right
way?*

A kilometer from the summit, the snow was six inches deep: we
had no choice but to ride in the slim tracks made by the team cars.
When one of those cars got stuck, we pedaled around it. But all
the cars behind it had to stop. Keeping me going was the thought
of Och at the summit, holding my musette of warm clothes for the
descent. But when I got there, I could tell something was wrong.
He hemmed and hawed and said, basically, "Sorry, bud. There
don't seem to be any more clothes."

I'd been sustained on the climb by the thought of bundling up.
So I let loose with a stream of expletives. Just then I heard a voice
calling my name from down the mountain. I turned and saw Mike
Hanley, one of our mechanics. He'd been in the 7-Eleven team car,
trapped behind the vehicle blocking the road. Suspecting I might
need them, he'd grabbed all the warm clothes he could find, then

set off in a dead run, catching me just in time. I thanked Mike then, and am thanking him now, for going above and beyond the call. And Och, while I'm at it, sorry about those f-bombs.

Make no mistake, it was *still* the most miserable descent of my life. I survived by braking as hard as I could — while still pedaling. The idea was to generate as much body heat as possible. Aside from hypothermia, my other main problem — everyone's main problem — was seeing where the hell we were going. This wasn't a video game: with minimum visibility, we had to get down a major mountain pass featuring plenty of potentially fatal drop-offs, and not that many guardrails. *If I go off one of these cliffs,* I thought to myself more than once, *they won't find me till next spring.*

My strategy for surviving the interminable switchbacks on the way to Bormio was to keep four bike-lengths between me and the rider in front of me. If he stacked it into a snowbank, I knew it was a hard turn and to ride it less aggressively. With my brakes compromised by the snow, I was forced on several corners to pull a foot out of the pedal and slow myself Fred Flintstone–style.

After twelve kilometers of descending, the snow turned back to sleet and finally just cold rain, which was an improvement.

Up ahead, Andy was passed by Erik Breukink and finished seven seconds behind the Dutchman, but he was OK with that. While he lost the stage, Andy's consolation prize was considerable: he became the first American ever to don the *maglia rosa* — the pink leader's jersey of the Giro.

After finishing the stage in a fantastic twenty-fourth place, Bob Roll was a giant popsicle, his heart rate a zombie-like twenty-four beats per minute. Deeply concerned, Max Testa found a warm room for him — the cramped area behind the stage where podium girls were primping. This arrangement pissed off the race promoter, but Max pulled rank. "I'm a doctor," he said, "and this guy is freezing. He needs to stay here." Roll was stretched out on the floor in a corner with a blanket over him.

When Max came back, Bob was miraculously recovered, sitting

up with coffee in hand, chatting up the girls. As Max put it, "He came around quite nicely."

On top of the mountain that day was John Wilcockson, of *Velo-News*. "So devastating was the freezing snow," he wrote, "that former Giro champions Roberto Visentini and Giuseppe Saronni were reduced to tears of pain. We watched Visentini coasting downhill like a rag doll at a quarter the speed he would normally descend. He stopped three times, once to don a padded ski jacket, another to drink hot tea, and then to have his frozen muscles rubbed back to life."

The local paper ran a front-page shot of Andy with his arm around Breukink, under the headline, "I Lupi del Gavia" — The Wolves of the Gavia.

"I'm not able to describe what my mind went through," is how Andy put it, years later. "It's the coldest I've ever been, the hardest thing I've ever done." He paused, not satisfied with that description, then said it another way: "It is by *far* the furthest my mind has pushed my body."

A quarter century later, Italian eyes light up at the mention of that Giro, and of that infamous day on the Gavia in particular. The *tifosi* still refer to Stage 14 of the '88 Giro as "Il Giorno Della Neve" — The Day of Snow. The widely chronicled tears of Visentini and Saronni earned the stage a second nickname: "The Day Grown Men Cried." A week later, Andy became the first non-European to win the Giro d'Italia. He remains so to this day.

The raced ended in Vittorio Veneto, an hour from the Adriatic Sea. We could've celebrated in Venice that night, or Verona — at any restaurant in Italy. Instead, we piled into our team cars, found the autostrada, and hammered west for nearly three hours, finally spilling out of our vehicles in Villa d'Almè. Bursting through the doors at the Bar Augusto, we were embraced like so many prodigal sons. And there, over the same table on which had once sat that one, sad little trophy, we raised to the ceiling a *maglia rosa* signed by Andy Hampsten, occupying its rightful place among the jerseys of Coppi, Gino Bartali, and Merckx — *I Grandi*. The Greats.

After hours of laughter and hearty food and good vino, we did not return to our cars. We made our way upstairs, to those cell-like rooms, then collapsed into the familiar, spartan bunks, yielding to deep sleep and the warm feeling of things coming full circle.

Writhing on an operating table in the fourth hour of brain surgery, the forty-nine-year-old version of me envied and begrudged the twenty-nine-year-old version of me that deep, uninterrupted slumber at the Bar Augusto.

Jaimie was working as fast as he could. He'd drilled two holes to access the subthalamic nucleus. Using that 3-D map as his guide, he'd threaded wires containing leads, or contacts, deep into my brain. These contacts would, at a later time, be modulated for frequency, amplitude, and pulse width. Even with all that incredibly precise mapping, Jaimie needed "eyes" inside my brain. That critical information was provided by my neurologist, the brilliant Dr. Helen Bronte-Stewart, whose passion for understanding how the brain controls movement first sprang from her background in classical and modern dance.

Helen helped guide Jaimie by listening to the "music" of my brain. Wearing specialized headphones, she monitored the different levels of static produced by different parts of the brain. At one point she noted that my STN was above average in size. Several "size" jokes ensued.

Five days later, I would be back on this table for a second surgery — phase three. The other ends of those wires would be dragged under my scalp, behind my right ear and down my neck, then attached to a battery pack roughly the size of the iPod classic. That device, a brain pacemaker designed by Medtronic, would live beneath the skin under my right collarbone. For some reason, I felt the need to name it. I settled on Bob. Two weeks after Bob came on board, we returned to the hospital for "programming," which Connie and I referred to as the Moment of Truth.

The leads send their electronic signals into the STN. The stimulation of that area is a finely tuned exercise that is part science, part intuition, part experience, and all magic. Without a superb programmer, the fine work of the surgeon is minimized greatly. There are thousands of possible variations of the settings. It was my good fortune to be working with Helen, one of the best in the world at what she does.

Before they screwed plastic covers over the dime-sized holes in my skull, then closed the incisions in my scalp with thirty-five surgical staples, the doctors took the hardware they'd installed on a kind of neurological shakedown cruise. To make sure they'd placed the leads in the "sweet spot," they switched on the current to see what would happen.

Immediately I felt this incredible calm, a wave of relaxation. An unclenching. Flipping that switch, Helen dissolved the armor that had encased me for the better part of a decade. My left hand, which had been in full tremor, became still.

It was a sublime moment — and oh so tantalizing, but I wasn't home free. Helen switched the power off: like hyenas, the symptoms came skulking back. The final phase of the DBS procedure — the programming — was still almost three weeks away. Until it was completed, we wouldn't know whether the surgery had been a success. But I was very, very encouraged.

I knew that deep brain stimulation couldn't cure me. Again, there is no known cure for Parkinson's. But it could ease my underlying symptoms. It would allow me to cut back on my consumption of pills, those tiny two-edged swords that gave me fleeting relief, but not without cost. DBS would help me sleep, restore my dreams. It would ease Connie's burden, even as it freed me to be more present in the lives of my children.

While I convalesced with friends in California, Taylor was

gearing up to ride in Europe with the national team. I was missing out on this critical period in his season, but this work of recovery was important. I so desperately wanted my life back. If it worked, I could follow Taylor to Beijing in August. If not, I'd be watching him on TV. I mean, by then, my symptoms were so pronounced, I had to think hard about eating in restaurants, let alone subjecting my Parkinson's bod to an eighteen-hour journey.

I guess, in a sense, beyond everything else, I had holes drilled in my head so I could go and see my son in his first Olympics. And, really, what better reason could there be?

17

— — —

The Light in Your Face
Just Came On Again

I T HAD BEEN two and a half weeks since that teasing, enticing glimpse — since Dr. Helen Bronte-Stewart flipped the switch, pulling back the curtain on the relief that *might* be in store for me once all the DBS hardware was in place and fired up. (Helen wasn't trying to give me a sneak preview — she and Jaimie needed to make sure those leads were well placed in my brain.) The tremor on my left side was stilled immediately. A wave of relief washed over me. Almost before I realized what had happened, she switched the current off. It was too early for me to enter that world.

Bob and I had seventeen days to get acquainted before the Moment of Truth. Working with a PDA-type device that she wielded like a maestro, Dr. Bronte-Stewart would then be free to tweak and fine-tune Bob's settings, to maximize the benefits of the surgery. The interim required patience.

There are a lot of neurosurgeons around the country who perform deep brain stimulation. They all have their own personal preferences. After phases two and three — drilling through the skull and placing the leads, then implanting the battery pack in the patient's chest — Dr. Henderson likes to give the brain a few weeks to recover before the Moment of Truth. He vetoed air travel immediately after surgery; the risk of infection, he felt, was too great.

Since it seemed impractical to drive a thousand miles home, just to turn around and drive back two weeks later, I relied on the support and hospitality of friends.

Connie flew home to be with our kids, while I decamped to Tiburon, in the North Bay. There, I was a guest of friends Carl and Candie Weissensee. During that time, Monique Petrov, a personal trainer and elite triathlete, provided generous time and support. My sister Alice flew out for a weekend to be with me. I felt the love and ease of one whose only job is to recover.

I also felt the pain in my ribs after catching a couple of hours of Robin Williams's standup act at the Throckmorton Theatre in Mill Valley. Seriously, I got to laughing so hard I thought I might bust a few of the sutures in my head. Connie and I met Williams during the mass-participation event at one of Lance Armstrong's Ride for the Roses. It was an exceptionally hot day, with a lot of dehydrated casualties along the side of the road. One of them was a squat, powerful, hirsute gentleman who took us up on our offer of assistance. "Connie and Davis helped me when I was cramping up and sweating like Elizabeth Taylor after a Mexican meal," he would later riff. "I was *not* lookin' good."

Since then, we've become friends, and Robin has become a generous supporter of the DPF. A few years ago, at a San Francisco fundraiser, he was auctioning off one of his road bikes when he noticed me sipping coffee.

"What are you doing, with Parkinson's, drinking coffee?" he asked, feigning shock. "That's a ballsy move!" I had little to no tremor that night, but still had problems with coffee spillage — because I was laughing so hard.

It was a kick catching his show in Mill Valley, going backstage, saying hi to him, taking off my baseball cap, allowing him to admire my recently shaved head, and the scars on my skull.

Physically I felt strong. I took daily hikes in the surrounding hills, which were just then coming alive in a riot of wildflowers. The special beauty of spring in Marin County, joined with the promise of my own imminent rebirth, filled me with a hope and optimism I had not known in years. In the same way I once looked forward to races, I was eager to get back to the hospital, to the instant when Helen would fire up the battery pack once and for all. Bring on the voltage.

I was going to have to earn that moment—was going to have to go through a bit of hell to get to heaven, much the same way I used to gut myself during a bike race so I could put my hands in the air at the end of it. For this final phase, I needed once again to be meds-free; Helen wanted to work with me in all my tremoring glory. So I spent another miserable night, lying on my left side, vibrating like a well-struck gong, pinning my left hand underneath myself in a largely futile attempt to keep it still. Several times I had to tell myself, *Suck it up. You can do this.*

And you know what? It helped. My background as a professional in pain management came in handy. *I might be shaking,* I told myself, *but at least I'm not* cold.

Despite getting no more than an hour or two of ragged sleep, I arose eager and excited on the morning of April 25, 2008. The day had arrived, at long last, for Helen to switch on the pacemaker and commence searching for the ideal settings. I was a whirling dervish when we arrived at the hospital. Before the programming, the doctors needed to record a baseline of my basic function, a process that, for this impatient sprinter, dragged on interminably. Finally, it was time for the Moment.

While Helen channel-surfed to define the parameters, I had a slew of odd reactions: jolts, tingles, tickling sensations. At one setting my thoughts evaporated, making intelligent conversation impossible. At another, my tongue felt grotesquely swollen, even though it wasn't. Helen kept surfing. Now I could neither open nor close my right hand. *Interesting!* And at another setting, my left foot began hopping of its own accord. *Please get it right,* I prayed to the gods of electrical currents.

Gradually, expertly, Helen zeroed in on the right settings—the sweet spot—probing, tweaking, until, in an *aha!* moment, it was as if I'd stepped out of a time machine. My muscles, taut and rigid for so long, unclenched. What coursed through me next was a wave of blissful, intoxicating relief, a cool breeze of relaxation.

"Look at this," Helen exclaimed, staring at my left hand. "He's got no tremor. It's a zero."

She was still tweaking the settings when I noticed that Connie was blinking back tears. "It's like you've been encased in armor all these years," she told me. "And the light in your face just came on again."

18

Beyond Beijing

*E*NCASED IN ARMOR.

Exactly.

More than the tremoring and the halting speech, I'd been worn down by a gathering sense of incarceration. I remember being reduced to tears by the film *The Diving Bell and the Butterfly*. It is the story of Jean-Dominique Bauby, a French magazine editor who was paralyzed by a stroke in his mid-forties. Diagnosed with "locked-in syndrome," he dictated a memoir by blinking his left eye, using the "butterfly" of his memory and imagination to escape the "diving bell" of his body.

Despite having far greater function than Bauby, I empathized strongly with his plight. In addition to the masking and loss of function, Parkinson's forces an entirely different personality on us. Where I had been gregarious, outgoing, vital, it imposed caution, reserve, self-consciousness. I worried about scattering my food in restaurants, flinging coins all over the counter in convenience stores. Instead of savoring meals, I ate with my head down, as quickly as I could. I lost the ease with which I had once glided through the world.

The rediscovery of that ease, the casting off of my armor with the flip of a switch—I count this as one of the miracles of my life, a notch below the sight of my children coming into the world. Sure, I was far from back to normal. But I was vastly improved.

I still have peaks and valleys: fantastic days, and days when I'm shaky and bummed out and kicked in the ass. (Such days, not surprisingly, come on the heels of days when I've pushed too hard, abused the gift.)

The DBS didn't cure me. It simply addressed my underlying symptoms. But the relief it's given me so far has been dramatic. Since the surgery, my voice is stronger, my diction clearer. My hands, which worked about as well as yours do if you did everything wearing oven mitts, work much better now. Walking is easier, although my balance is still a bit off. I'm sleeping much more deeply. Not perfectly, but sans tremor. I'm recovering myself, is what it comes down to.

Walking out of the hospital that afternoon, I saw the world in a different light—through the prism of this second chance, this new lease. And it was beautiful. For the first few days, I kept waiting for the effects to wear off, like the medicine always did. I caught myself worrying that this was all a dream from which I would soon awaken. I did have minor ups and downs, with much-muted tremors coming and going. But they occurred within a far more limited range.

Over the next few days I felt lighter, as if a burden had been lifted. In a sense, it had: I was free to shed a hundred habits and learned behaviors and coping mechanisms accumulated over the previous decade. I didn't need to choose the clothes I wore based on whether the pockets would accommodate my shaking hand. For the first time in eight years, I could eat sushi with chopsticks.

No one knows how long the effects of the DBS will last. Dr. Henderson had told me he believed it could turn back the clock on my PD by five years or more. I intended, from the beginning, to milk it for much longer than that. Who better than I to wring the maximum benefit from the surgery?

You see where this is going. The doctors and nurses emphasized the importance of taking it easy, being gentle with myself. Even as I nodded earnestly through these lectures, I could not alter my nature, which is to find my limits and promptly exceed them. And so I found out the hard way that recovering from brain surgery is not like having a cast removed from a broken wrist. It is not an invitation to go out and push yourself to the nth degree. I pushed myself to that limit, and quickly found myself in a world of hurt.

After the 2008 track worlds in Manchester, Taylor flew home to Colorado for a few weeks to catch up and finish his schoolwork, then jetted back to Europe for a stage race in Switzerland. NBC raised the level of excitement at the race by sending a film crew, and Taylor did not disappoint, winning the time trial in his white world-champion skin suit. After returning to the States for the Olympic Trials and some extensive track work (where, in the course of riding three successive 3k pursuits, he set a junior world record in each one), he was ready to *really* start traveling.

Start traveling? In 2008 alone he'd flown to Europe and back three times. But yes, now began the big loop of the planet. We scheduled a week in Marostica. It would be a convenient intermediate stop, we figured, a place to shake off the jet lag in familiar territory.

What I didn't foresee was how difficult the conditions would be. The combination of stifling heat, no AC, jet lag, and lousy sleep flung open the door for my symptoms to come raging back.

Already kicked in the ass, shaking harder than at any time since the DBS, I found myself further in the red when, after a mad scramble through the Frankfurt airport, we missed our connection to Cape Town, site of the world junior championships. It was our bad luck that the UCI had chosen 2008 as the year to let South Africa host the junior worlds. Granted, Taylor was the only athlete in the bunch who was also going to Beijing, but it added an additional ten thousand miles of travel to an already overly ambitious journey.

Taylor wanted to defend his junior world time trial title, and win a second title on the track. He succeeded on the track but failed to defend his TT title, taking bronze instead. It was a long, unsettling trip to a winter climate (southern hemisphere in July means winter), and not exactly conducive to the prep he needed for Beijing. But it was his last year as a junior, and he would not even consider skipping this event.

By the time we got to Cape Town, after the delays and reroutings, I was struggling. Where the heat had undone me in Italy, South Africa's bone-chilling cold sapped my energy—that and the anxiety we felt when Taylor's track bike failed to show up with the rest of his luggage. (It arrived the day before the race.) Adding to that distress, a police officer was shot and killed right in front of our hotel, which we'd assumed to be in a safe area. We heard the gunfire. That put us all on edge: it suddenly became clear that Kelsey's solo runs in the vicinity, Connie's rides alone, and my going for walks with a big camera around my neck had been not-so-hot ideas. Nearby, we later learned, Henk Boeve had been mugged for his camera. The father of Dutch junior rider Mats Boeve, Henk was also the guy I outsprinted for my first Tour de France stage win, in 1986. Cycling is a small world.

We did have one brilliant day at the Cape of Good Hope, which lived up to its name. It replenished us and provided a half day of solace. Apart from being chased by a few baboons, we were blissfully content to watch the pounding surf until sunset and then drive like hell out of there.

For my part, I was cranky, exhausted, and frankly terrified that, by overtaxing myself, I'd undone the beneficial effects of the deep brain stimulation. I had pushed too hard, abused the gift, flown too close to the sun. I'd broken Bob. My trip to Beijing was suddenly in doubt.

I was a burden on the family and a source of anxiety that our young Olympian didn't need. After talking it over with Connie, we decided that, rather than proceed to France and the velodrome at Bordeaux, I'd detour home to Boulder, have my settings readjusted, get some rest, then reevaluate. She quickly rerouted me, and I flew home with Kelsey.

After a few decent nights of sleep in Colorado, my symptoms had largely abated, to my vast relief. I was terrifically encouraged after a visit to my Denver-based neurologist, Dr. Olga Klepitskaya.

"I went on this very ambitious trip," I explained to her. "It was very hot. I slept poorly. And . . . I had access to a bicycle." I sounded like a junkie admitting to a relapse.

She noticed that I was favoring my left ankle, obligating me to explain that I'd badly sprained it several weeks earlier . . . while doing backflips on the trampoline behind our house. (Backflips? Yeah. I grew up with a trampoline. In its own curious way, soaring and flipping have always freed me, for those fleeting midair moments, from the armor.) Olga took that news in stride, which gratified me.

After noting that my speech seemed "a little bit sticky," she tweaked Bob's settings a tiny bit, inspected my gait as I strode up and down the corridor, then tweaked some more.

"No one will believe you are a patient here," she said. With a smile, Olga wished Taylor luck, and reminded me to respect my body's limits on the upcoming journey.

It stands to reason that I would have learned that lesson, once and for all, following that big scare in South Africa. Yet, in the intervening years, I've needed several refresher courses. (I'm thinking, in particular, of the winter morning, after a couple of hours of cross-country skiing, that I challenged Kelsey to a sprint. She immediately bolted to a ten-yard lead. In pursuit, I missed a pole stroke and jackhammered cranium-first into the hard-packed snow. When my vision cleared, Connie calmly asked me a rhetorical question, having witnessed the debacle: "How could you be so f——g stupid?")

The truth is, I'm willing to pay a little bit, on the back end, to live my life more fully in this moment. The fact that I was going to be tapped out and drained at the end of the trip couldn't keep me from flying to Beijing.

Each venue at the Beijing Olympics had its own distinct personality, from the oddball latticework of the Bird's Nest (aka Beijing National Stadium) to the bubble-wrapped Water Cube, where swimming phenom Michael Phelps ruled, to the Laoshan Velodrome, which looked for all the world like some flying saucer that had landed on the western outskirts of the city.

The infield within the oval was a mini-Olympics in its own right: a maze of open cubicles containing bikes and riders from scores of nations. It was fitting that our family's most memorable moments in China took place in a building that looked like a spaceship. The Twenty-ninth Olympiad was but the latest stop on a wild, improbable journey that, though not interstellar, had taken us to most corners of the planet.

To cut down on my time away from home, I watched the opening ceremony from our living room in Boulder. There was T, striding around the track at the Bird's Nest, his Team USA–issued Ralph Lauren white beret pulled rakishly low, while he cut up with the American gymnasts and palled around with members of the men's basketball team.

Little did I know that it would be easier to watch my son on television in Colorado than it would be to see him in person once I arrived in Beijing. The International Olympic Committee and the need for security in the Olympic Village had made it extremely difficult for Connie and me and Taylor's coach, Neal Henderson, to spend *any* time with him before he raced. That wasn't good for Taylor, who, it should be remembered, had done only nine pursuit races in his life to that point, and had just turned eighteen. He was accustomed to one system of preparation, with Neal and Connie and me helping to organize his equipment and guiding his preparation—basically troubleshooting for him. Due to the maddening inflexibility of the rules, we could barely get close enough to speak to him. Suddenly, he was completely disconnected from his usual support structure. It was as if he was on the other side of the Berlin Wall.

The day of T's race, Neal was allowed into the Olympic Village to see him before the event. On the day after—the day of his second ride—we handed in our passports outside the Olympic Village, were herded through several security checkpoints, and finally were granted a brief audience with our son. Taylor appeared relaxed, but was clearly distracted, and mentioned more than once the American contingent of female gymnasts, who had taken up quarters one floor directly above him. Taylor and gymnast Shawn Johnson struck up a friendship. Connie and I glanced at each other, having the same thought: *Where is his head at?* We went to the Olympic mess hall, where a stunning collection of elite athletes were chowing down. We even walked by Michael Phelps, who was casually striding back to his own dorm room after lunch. The Olympic Village was a fantastical spectrum of athletes, a truly beautiful world unto itself.

From our seats at the velodrome that night, it was tough to read T's mood. Never the bashful type, Connie busied herself deputizing our fellow spectators in Section 113, granting them instant membership in the Taylor Phinney Fan Club. "That rider is my son," she announced, loudly, as T spun past on a warm-up lap. "When it's his turn to ride, please cheer!"

T would need all the help he could get. Eighteen riders were in the event; only eight would advance to the next round. Taylor was paired against Volodymyr "the Dude" Dudya, the Ukrainian who'd finished the season ranked first in the World Cup standings.

The youngest rider in the field, Taylor went out like the newbie he is, blazing through his first lap in 20.3 seconds, the fastest

opening lap of the night. The problem was, he had fifteen more to
go. Having taken an early lead on the Dude, he started looking labored in the final kilometer.

After gutting out a personal-best 4:22.860, the kid nearly collapsed after dismounting his bike — atypically, for him. His time
slotted him into fifth place, ahead of some huge names in the
sport. Ominously for Taylor, two pairs of higher-seeded pursuit-
ers had yet to compete. But in the next race, David O'Loughlin
and Bradley McGee — an Aussie who took silver in the event four
years before — cracked like maple bats. The posting of their official times, slower than Taylor's, triggered a celebration that rippled
from twenty or so family and friends comprising Team Taylor to
the farthest reaches of Section 113. Taylor had accomplished Goal
No. 1 — he would ride in the second round.

The next day, Taylor went up against a New Zealander named
Hayden Roulston, one of the veteran kiwis he'd befriended during that July training block in France. Taylor had been tearing
up the track at the velodrome in Bordeaux, riding faster than he
ever had in his life. Somehow, between the time he left France and
took the start line in Laoshan, he was four or five seconds slower.
Where did that time go? I think he lost a second or two wandering
around the Olympic Village for a couple of days in shock and awe.
The disruption of his training and race-day routines didn't help,
and participating in the opening ceremony will be a definite no-
no if he ever gets a second chance at the Olympics. And we now
acknowledge that he spent too much time circumnavigating the
globe, training for and racing the pursuit, not enough time getting
hard road miles in his legs (a theory that would be vindicated at
the world championships the following spring).

Taylor has always had plenty of speed, but he came into the
games short on base training miles, and it showed. In his second
Olympic ride, he was trounced by Roulston, the kiwi, who then
took silver behind gold medalist Bradley Wiggins of Great Britain.
Taylor's final placing was seventh.

Recalling my own Olympic disappointment, and the lengthy funk into which it plunged me, Connie and I made it a point to emphasize to Taylor how fast and far he'd come in six months. He said all the right things but, as we would later find out, he definitely took a big helping of regret home with him.

That wasn't a huge surprise to me. Ultimately, as a competitor, you live and die by your results. Very few athletes at these games had more fun than my son, whether he was striking Zoolander poses at the opening ceremony, or spearheading the "Beijing Airlift" in the Village. (That mercy mission entailed tossing Snickers bars to the balcony above his for his new friends on the US gymnastics team, who were forbidden to eat them.) Bottom line: it was a missed opportunity.

"This is not the end of the journey," Connie emphasized as we relaxed in the stands after that race. "It's the beginning." Ever upbeat, she'd also pointed out that, like Taylor, she'd placed seventh in *her* first Olympics. "Great," came T's reply. "Now all I have to do is switch sports, train for twelve years, then I can get a medal, too."

He'd experienced a ton of success, right away. It wasn't the worst thing in the world for him to be served a bit of humble pie—to see how hard he would have to work to reach Wiggins's level. In the end, it didn't take as long as we thought.

Connie never had an Olympic hangover, transitioning with her customary grace from the top step of the podium into the next phase of her life. My Olympic hangover was time-delayed. It kicked in a month or so after the Los Angeles Games. Taylor's Olympic hangover hit him pretty much the day he got back from Beijing.

His plan had been to fly home after his last race. But his new friend Shawn Johnson was sticking around for the closing ceremony, so Taylor changed his flight. He seemed a tad unfocused when he got home and, for the first time, was free from school (he had in fact graduated in June). The Olympics had been his raison d'être, his polestar. When the games were over, he entered a rudderless, aimless phase, much of which he spent figuring out ways he could connect with a certain four-foot, nine-inch gymnast. After a month or so of this drift, I began to wonder if he hadn't lost his motivation.

In early September, Taylor was planning a road trip to Oakland, where Shawn was performing. On the way back, he wanted to make a stop in Las Vegas to see his friend Danny Summerhill ride in a cyclocross race. Without coming across as too much of a wet blanket, I was trying to talk him out of the trip. Around this time, I got a text from an old friend in Austin, Texas.

"Is Taylor under contract?" he asked. Taylor, in fact, was nearing the end of his final season with the Garmin-Chipotle-sponsored junior program.

"Not yet," I texted back.

"I'll call you," Lance replied.

A few weeks earlier, Armstrong had been in the news for finishing second in the Leadville 100, a lung-searing, hundred-mile mountain bike race contested in the Colorado Rockies, at an altitude of ten-thousand-plus feet. His participation in the "Race Across the Sky" fueled rumors that he was considering a comeback — rumors that turned out to be true. Lance was kicking back in Austin with a few members of his inner circle, plotting his comeback, when Taylor's name came up. "That kid is going to win a gold medal in London in 2012," Lance declared. "We need to get him on a Trek bicycle."

Having closely followed Taylor's career, Lance recognized his talent and potential. To catch up with Taylor — they hadn't talked since the summer of 2005 — Lance invited him to Aspen for a five-day block of high-altitude training. Thus did his post-Olympic drift come to an abrupt close. Taylor was instantly refocused.

They spent some quality time together in the Rockies, getting reacquainted, taking the measure of each other. I didn't expect my son to be intimidated. But I was a bit surprised by his ain't-no-big-thing attitude, his ease in the company of the King. At a high-end sushi joint in Aspen one night, the seven-time Tour winner tried to rattle T's cage. He'd scheduled some core work for both of them with his personal trainer, Peter Park, the next morning. "He's sharpening his knives right now," Lance warned T. "He's going to shred you."

Looking up from his iPhone, every eye at the table on him, Taylor deadpanned, "Do I look worried?" Everyone, Lance included, broke up.

On September 24, 2008, at the Clinton Global Initiative in midtown Manhattan, Armstrong officially announced his comeback. Fleshing out the details of his return to racing, he spoke of his desire to help "develop young cyclists in the US." He announced that he and Trek had decided to start a team for cyclists under the age of twenty-three (U23), and that Taylor — "clearly the best and the brightest" — would be its centerpiece. To direct the squad, Armstrong hired T's old friend from the '05 Tour, Axel Merckx.

There stood my son, behind Armstrong and to his left, smiling, sporting the suit we'd bought him the day before at Men's Wearhouse, unfazed in the extreme, his expression saying: Yeah, this is working out pretty much the way I expected. I only saw Taylor look a tiny bit apprehensive when Armstrong described him as "the future of American cycling."

The next day's *New York Times* referred to Taylor as "the next Lance Armstrong." As he told a magazine reporter, "There's not going to be a next Lance Armstrong. But I am the next Taylor Phinney. And that might end up being pretty good."

On a misty morning the following February, I found myself riding shotgun in a team follow car, rolling past stately oaks and ponderosa pines in Sonoma County, California. Forty feet ahead was a pair of riders: a tan, ripped thirty-something beside a tall, pale *espoir* — a young pro.

As they spun and bantered up the road, I looked on with pride and a small measure of melancholy. The older rider was Armstrong, of course. Beside him was Taylor, who only yesterday, it seemed, I was pulling to preschool on a tagalong bike; videotaping as he launched off ramps in the cul-de-sac behind our house. Now he was up the road having a bro-down with the most famous cyclist in the world. I smiled, even as I couldn't help thinking, *That used to be me.*

That used to be me, setting the pace for Taylor, cajoling him up climbs, parceling out insights earned over the course of my own career. That was before my life was rerouted by the Body Snatcher. Cruising behind those two in the follow car during this preseason training camp, I reflected on how blessed Taylor is to be learning his craft from one of the greatest riders ever. I also reflected on how Lance — quite unintentionally — had changed the dynamic between my son and me.

Is it possible to be grateful to and feel threatened by the same person at the same time? Where I was once Taylor's main go-to guy for questions on cycling, on girls, on life, I'd been superseded by a certain Texan. It didn't help that, even post-DBS, Parkinson's still tended to gum up my cognitive function; that, depending on the day, it could take me a few extra seconds, or longer, to assemble thoughts and sentences. And while he has been incredibly considerate and loving throughout my illness, there were times when Taylor exhibited as much patience as your average eighteen-year-old. I'd be driving a point home — "If you're racing a tight circuit on a wet day, you want to slightly decrease . . ." — and he'd interrupt. "I know, Dad. Less tire pressure, I know."

Axel was in the follow car with me that morning, driving just behind Lance and Taylor. It soon become apparent to me that there was something out of whack with T's position; he couldn't get comfortable in his saddle. We called him back to the car, lowered the seat post, pushed the saddle back, then sent him on his way. I continued to tweak his position. Afterward, Axel and I tinkered with T's saddle, making micro-adjustments, discussing bike-fit theory, and basically geeking out like a couple of bike nerds. Taylor's gratitude was heartfelt, and I left the camp feeling a little more helpful, relevant, needed. The incident served as a reminder that no matter how many coaches and consultants he had, I'm the one with the mental Polaroid of how my son is supposed to look on his machine. In addition to having a keen eye for his position, my jobs include tinkerer in chief, triple-checking the setup on his various bikes, and dealing with company reps to make sure his equipment is up to snuff.

Two days later I dropped him off at the San Francisco airport. Taylor was bound for a World Cup track event in Copenhagen, where he would crush a field of veteran riders, in the process destroying a thirteen-year-old American record. Standing in the international terminal at SFO, he enveloped me in a hug and told me, "Man, I'm really going to *miss* you!" I didn't feel remotely extraneous.

In phone calls and Skype conversations over the next few days, Taylor told me he was riding some breathtakingly fast training laps. He had a target time in mind. He wanted to go 4:19, three seconds faster than his personal best. But the air in the velodrome was cooler than usual, which meant the rides would be slightly slower. His Team USA coaches advised him to shoot for a more realistic goal.

He thanked them for that counsel, then ignored it. "I'm gonna go *at least* 4:19," he said.

I was alone in a hotel room in Sacramento on Friday, February 13, when my phone vibrated. It was just after 5 P.M. in Copenhagen, where Taylor had finished his first race. Jim Miller of USA Cycling was texting a rhetorical question: "How about 4:15?"

It was a text that took my breath away, literally, and brought tears to my eyes.

What on earth got into him? How do you slice seven seconds off your personal-best time? It was the third-fastest pursuit ever

ridden. Where was that ride when he needed it, in Beijing the previous August?

The truth is, Taylor had been fueled by his Olympic failure. Between Beijing and Copenhagen, something clicked in his mind.
While he and Lance had their share of light moments, Taylor also
got a firsthand look at the way the Texan approached the business
of bike racing: his focus, his discipline, his dedication, his belief
in himself. Taylor understands his physical gifts. What he came to
understand, over the winter, was that at the highest levels of competition, the difference between winning and losing, or winning
and breaking records, is mental.

With that one ride, Taylor made a giant leap, from a wunder-
kind with huge potential to a young man who was ready to fulfill
that potential. Six weeks later, in his qualifying ride at the world
championships in Pruszkow, Poland, he shaved another tenth of
a second off his American record. That night, he would ride for
the world title. And so it came to pass that I stood stock-still in
the southeast corner of my living room — the four-square-foot area
of my house in which my cell-phone carrier is least likely to drop
a call — riveted by Connie's track-side account of Taylor's come-
from-behind effort in the final against the gifted young Aussie,
Jack Bobridge:

"C'mon T, c'mon! Go! Go! Go!" After trading the lead over
the first 2k, he trailed halfway through the race. "Oh, shoot, he's
down." Then, a rally . . . "OK, they're about even . . . Now Taylor's up on him. He's up! He's further up! He's pulling it out! HE'S
PULLING AWAY!" Then, after a cruel pause that lasted an eter-
nity: "YOUR SON'S WORLD CHAMPION!"

He was world champion, at the age of eighteen, in a discipline
few people outside the cycling world knew anything about. The
question was, would his prowess carry over to the road? Our old
friend, the journalist John Wilcockson, had taken a subtle shot at
Taylor, describing him (inaccurately) as the best-known bike racer
who'd never won a road race. As a follow-up to the track worlds,

Taylor had focused his early season around a prestigious one-day event: the U23 Paris-Roubaix, a slightly scaled down, 170-kilometer version of the best-known, most-feared one-day race in the world. The Hell of the North, as Paris-Roubaix is known, takes riders over twenty-six sections of jarring, irregular cobbles. When it rains during Paris-Roubaix—and it usually does—the cobbles become slick with a combination of mud and oil and the ordure of animals that have traversed them for centuries and do so to this day. Roubaix is a crashfest and a bloodbath of which I have only painful memories.

This aversion to—or bad luck on—the cobbles seemed to run in the family—or so I'd begun to suspect two years earlier. In 2007 Taylor took the start in the junior version of Paris-Roubaix. He had a less than auspicious day. After three crashes, one bike change, a bent chain ring, and a punctured tire, he found himself on the side of the road, waiting for the broom wagon. Standing in the back of that support vehicle (whose driver, memorably, offered his teenaged passengers a shot of whiskey), he couldn't help but eavesdrop on a group of Italian riders, who'd also pulled out of the race, and who were shocked when this gangly American started speaking to them in fluent Italian.

I was disappointed for him that day, but struck by what he vowed shortly thereafter: "I have a new lifelong goal. One day, I want to be first across the finish line in Paris-Roubaix."

On the eve of the U23 version of the race, he sent me an SOS text in the middle of the night. He had a sore throat—felt a cold coming on. Did I have any advice? (I didn't get the message until the following morning, by which time he'd Googled "exercising with a cold." As he later told Connie, "I got permission to race from the Internet.") Reading that text at 6 A.M. Boulder time, I worried that he might not even finish the race. Oddly, being under the weather had a positive effect on him. Careful not to waste any energy, he rode the perfect race, staying up front, and out of trouble.

That morning, Connie and I participated in an event called

"Ride 2 Victory," a fundraiser for my foundation. The R2V is best known for its easygoing, friendly vibe, and for the killer breakfast put out by chef Bradford Heap at the Colterra Restaurant in Niwot, Colorado—a half mile from where Bob Cook and I won our respective categories at the 1977 Colorado state championship. The R2V field of several hundred riders included at least two dozen who'd competed with Connie and me throughout our careers. Dale Stetina and Ron Kiefel were there, as was—to my surprise—Alexi Grewal, who gave me a big hug and introduced me to his eleven-year-old son, Elijah, who knocked out the forty-miler, so far as I could tell, without breaking a sweat.

So I was feeling nostalgic and embraced and suffused with a sense of things coming full circle *before* I took the call from Axel Merckx, who was standing five thousand miles away, in the infield of the velodrome in Roubaix, France. "How'd it go?" I asked, with some trepidation. He answered by handing the phone to Taylor, who said, "Guess who won Paris-Roubaix!"

"NO WAY!" I shouted. I put the phone to my chest and yelled, "TAYLOR PHINNEY JUST WON THE UNDER-TWENTY-THREE PARIS-ROUBAIX!" This great cheer went up around us and rippled outward. We rode a wave of congratulations and good will all the way to the finish that day, and beyond.

Taylor had been part of an eleven-rider group that reached the Roubaix velodrome ahead of the rest of the field. The race ends with two laps on a banked oval—a decided advantage, in retrospect, to the world champion in the individual pursuit. Taylor attacked with half a lap remaining, and won going away.

Behind him that day, riding shotgun in the follow car beside Axel, was Axel's father, the greatest bike racer of all time. A friend later texted me what Eddy Merckx said about Taylor after watching him win that race.

The exact quote was: "I have never seen an eighteen-year-old that strong."

19

As Good as It Gets

'D HEARD THE voice before, but it had never spoken so clearly. *I don't want to do this anymore.*

I was in a long line of riders suffering up some nameless grade in the Alleghenies or Blue Ridge Mountains in the first week of the 1993 Tour DuPont. The pace was punishing; a blazing sun had softened the macadam, making the going even tougher. I was hot, I was tired. I hurt.

I was in my third season with the Coors Light team, 7-Eleven having pulled the plug on its sponsorship after the '90 season. Len Pettyjohn, the Coors director, preferred to focus more on the domestic racing scene, which suited me. I was ready to stop spending so much of my life in Europe, away from my family. I was ready to stop suffering for a living.

I made a big splash early on for Coors Light, winning the opening stage of the '91 Tour DuPont. In Philly three weeks later, I won the US national championship at the 156-mile CoreStates USPRO road race. Later that summer, I was victorious in a well-known stage race called the Fitchburg Longsjo Classic, in Massachusetts. I won it by attacking on the toughest stage, which ends atop Wachusett Mountain.

Defending my title at Fitchburg in '92, I jumped into an early breakaway on the road to that mountain. Our pace line consisted of half a dozen guys, and we were *booking*. We thought. I was taking long, ripping pulls in my 53-12, trying to tear the other guys' legs off, even as I left something in the tank for the climb up Wachusett.

We were still thirty miles from the finish when something odd happened. As we labored up a short climb, one of the guys in our group, a US national team rider named Darren Baker, stopped working. He was merely sitting on the back, enjoying the benefits of the draft we were creating, but refusing to take a pull himself. Back then, the US national team was one of the few squads in the world using race radios. Baker had just gotten some news in his earpiece.

Soon there was a split in the caravan of cars behind us. They were making way for a rider who'd bridged up from the pack—a remarkable feat, considering that the main bunch was over three minutes behind us.

Lance Armstrong was twenty years old, and he barely glanced at us as he blew our doors off that day. He slowed *just* enough for Baker to catch his slipstream, then they were off. I turned to Irishman Paul McCormack and asked, "What just happened?"

I had seen the future of American cycling, and I was not a part of it. Lance won that stage up Wachusett Mountain by something like four minutes. And so, at the end of the following season, I listened to that voice. Eighteen years after that high school teacher told me I could never make a living as a bike racer, I retired from bike racing.

But what a life it was! I have little doubt that my chosen profession, which called on me to subject my body to cruel and unusual punishment on a regular basis for the better part of two decades, played a role in my coming down with Parkinson's disease. (Or maybe it was just the goddamn fumes wafting around our basement while my dad patched tires and developed pictures.)

I have even less doubt, had I known my fate ahead of time, that I would have changed a thing. I loved my life. I loved the Life. It's different now; my life still finds me suffering, still finds me traveling, and even still finds me in front of large audiences — now in my quest to spread the message of the Davis Phinney Foundation: Every Victory Counts.

It never got any better than the 1988 Coors Classic, which spanned two weeks and took riders 1,070 miles across the American West. Its multiple mountain stages made Andy Hampsten the odds-on prerace favorite. But I felt strong from the start, winning the prologue up to San Francisco's Coit Tower. Four days later, the peloton was zipping along Highway 50, the amethyst expanse of Lake Tahoe to our left. Just ahead, the only stiff climb of the stage. Andy, as expected, was leading the race. "Let's go!" I told him. It was time for him to attack.

"No, *you* go," he replied. "Everyone will chase if I'm with you."

As Hampsten explained to the *New York Times*, "It was a tactical move. I was the leader and everyone was following me. So I called their bluff." It may have been a tactical move, but it was also a selfless one. Andy was saying he didn't care who won, as long as it was a member of our team. He was being a mensch, paying me back for the work I'd done for him at the Giro.

The breakaway group was eight riders strong, including Alexi Grewal, who was riding for a squad sponsored by Crest. (Scanning highlights from that race on the Red Zinger/Coors Classic DVD, it's tough to say which is more regrettable: Crest's uniforms — those guys looked like rolling tubes of toothpaste — Andy's bouffant do, or the mini-mullet ponytails sported by Jeff Pierce and . . . me.)

Also in the break was Alex Stieda, who'd ministered to me and told me off-color jokes in the ambulance on that bloody day the previous April. With Andy and the boys blocking behind us, we did some serious damage, carving out a five-minute lead at one point, and reshuffling the standings. I outsprinted a Dutch rider named Gerrit de Vries for the stage win, but Stieda moved into the lead, and I was thrilled for him. He was a strong, selfless rider who deserved some podium time.

A few days later we were in Aspen for a sixty-mile circuit race. This was Grewal's turf—his father ran a high-end bike shop right in town. He wanted this stage badly—but not as badly as I wanted to beat him. Alan McCormack and I attacked on the ninth circuit of this thirty-seven-lap race, and stayed away for forty-five miles. Three hundred yards from the line, I shook my Irish friend to take my fourth stage win of this race.

Alexi paid me back the next day, attacking on the road to 12,095-foot Independence Pass. Deep-fried and dropped on early slopes of that mountain, I was patiently paced back to the main group by Roy Knickman. Alexi and several other strong climbers had four minutes on us at the top of the pass, but we didn't panic. Drilling it hard on the descent and on into the town of Leadville, our group caught the breakaway in time for me to collect the midrace sprint bonus.

By winning that intermediate sprint way back in Leadville, I'd earned enough bonus seconds to dethrone my teammate—the guy who had unhesitatingly stopped racing in order to be by my side at the hospital. I apologized to Alex, who told me not to be ridiculous. "Dave, you grew up on this race," he said. "Now you're in position to win it in your own backyard!"

The race had come down to Grewal and me. It was tense between the Crest guys and us. There's footage from that Aspen circuit race of Alexi's kid brother, Rishi, veering thirty feet across the road to stiff-arm some blue-jerseyed opponent, after which the Grewals commenced pointing and screaming at the rider. Those guys were competitors. They hated losing, and they were losing by a little every day.

After I took the lead, Alexi was asked if he was frustrated. "I'm not frustrated at all," he snapped at the reporter. "Why the hell should I be frustrated?"

By the end of the fourteenth stage, Alexi's frustration had given way to resignation. "Crest is the second-best team in the United States," he remarked after collapsing at the end of the Morgul-Bismarck stage, his last, best chance to unseat me. "7-Eleven is one of the best teams in the world."

Ron Kiefel became the fifth 7-Eleven rider to win a stage of this race by taking the last circuit race in Boulder. Four of us had at one point held the race lead. But I held it on the last day, and won a shiny new BMW convertible on top of the other cash prizes. Teams typically split their winnings among them, but our team — which had succeeded despite its humble beginnings — had Jim Ochowicz to thank for defining us, and we thanked him by giving him the keys and the title to that beemer, which he still maintains and drives to this day.

Humming along in a protective cocoon of red and green riders during the final stage, a criterium around the Colorado campus, I couldn't help but allow my mind to wander back to another Sunday afternoon, thirteen years earlier, in this same city. That was the day I'd first seen a pro bike race — the day I'd glimpsed my path in the world.

Take the profile of all the climbs I've ridden — and descents I've scorched — and print out a thousand copies. Lay those pages end to end, and you are looking at my journey over thirteen years, from the wide-eyed kid watching the Red Zinger through a fence, to the scarred vet on the top step of the podium on the last day of the last Coors Classic. My rise in this sport, which reached its apex in the summer of '88, was gradual, interrupted, the opposite of meteoric. My career, like a lot of careers, consisted of a series of climbs, or victories (some literal, some moral), each followed by an inevitable dip (the flat tire in Louisville, the Olympic disappointment, my face-first flight through a pane of glass in Belgium). My setbacks, always temporary, were followed by a literal or figurative standing up, taking inventory (anything broken?), scrubbing the gravel out of my road rash, and getting back in the saddle. In this halting, unglamorous fashion — trial followed by error; two steps forward, one back; by piling gain on incremental gain — I managed to attain heights previously unscaled.

It is this way in life. Hard work is key, but so is confronting and challenging weaknesses. It was infinitely more rewarding to fine-tune and nurture my strengths, but I had to work on all aspects to grow and improve.

And I was mentally tough. I tried to turn every reversal of fortune into a teachable moment, then used that lesson, that hard-earned experience, to get a little farther up the mountain the next time. Or I just got pissed off, and used my anger as fuel. That works, too, sometimes. Often I just had to get over myself. Accept that good comes with bad. But as long as the good moments are more frequent than the bad, the overall trajectory was always pointing upward. If this resonates with you, I know why: It's an experience not unique to sports. And it's the mindset that has served me so well in my struggle with PD, where I work hard for and savor the good days and do my best to minimize the bad.

Standing on that podium at the University of Colorado, waving to a crowd of some thirty thousand people, it never crossed my mind (and why should it have?) that I was hovering, in that moment, a month after my twenty-ninth birthday, at my professional apex. For me, winning the '88 Coors Classic was as good as it was going to get.

If my rise in the sport was the opposite of meteoric, Taylor's has been the opposite of mine. Of course, bike racing has brought him low, kicked his butt, reduced him to tears, and sent him to the hospital. Crashing heavily in the Cascade Cycling Classic in Oregon in late July 2009, he suffered a severe concussion that effectively ended his season.

He absorbed a more severe blow to his plans in December of the same year, when the UCI recommended to the International

Olympic Committee that the individual pursuit—in which Taylor was reigning world champion—be dropped from the Olympic schedule, a turn of events that caught us totally off-guard. Despite the eloquent, superbly reasoned arguments against such a move put forth by John Wilcockson in *VeloNews,* and despite a "Save the Pursuit" Internet petition signed by close to five thousand people, the IOC rubber-stamped the UCI's recommendation, in one fell swoop removing T's best chance at a medal in the 2012 London Olympics.

The pursuit event gave Taylor a world stage, it gave him the opportunity to develop and flourish. When it was pulled away, doors did not close—they opened. It's always that way in sports and even more so in life. Happiness comes from the pursuits within your life—whether those dreams are lofty Olympic ambitions or those smaller everyday goals that I now set for myself. In fact, happiness occurs most often in those moments when I'm pursuing nothing more than allowing myself to be absorbed in the moment. Just being.

Kelsey, Connie, and I found ourselves between Bike Camps in June of 2009, exploring the area around Lucca, Italy, and soaking up the *dolce vita.* It occurred to us that if we drove five hours to France just west of Mont Blanc, we could see Taylor racing with the US national team. It was a long drive, and a long shot. But it was Father's Day, and so I made the call: *Andiamo!* Let's go!

We arrived Saturday in time to watch Taylor suffer up the wicked south side of the Col de la Madeleine, having paced his teammate Tejay van Garderen to the base. The guys slogged to the finish in a cold, driving rain, bringing back memories I'd long since buried. Bike racing is hard, and then it gets harder. After crossing the line, the lads were all forced to ride downhill two miles to their hotels. They arrived shivering.

We'd been lucky to find a tiny mountain pension with dorm-style rooms and a great little restaurant that dished up a super-rustic raclette (warmed cheese and potatoes). Pure happiness.

Sunday's route took riders up the ribbon of road pedaled by my father thirteen years earlier, from the valley town of Saint-Jean-de-Maurienne to the top of the Col de la Croix de Fer. Connie dropped off Kelsey and me and our bikes about twelve miles from the summit, then drove ahead to park and wait for us, and for Taylor. Kels and I were chatting away, still a half mile or so from the summit, when a small caravan of official cars and motorcycles came honking through. Taylor's race had arrived! We pulled over to watch the spectacle.

For all his gifts, my muscular, six-feet-four-inch son is not a natural climber. Still, he wanted very much to ride past his family with the front group. He'd been close for miles, but was dangling just off the back of that elite bunch of perhaps a dozen riders when he noticed us. His breath was ragged, his suffering palpable, yet he flashed us a smile.

The iron cross for which this col is named isn't so heavy or imposing as it might sound. The "Croix" is actually just a wrought-iron outline of a cross, mounted on a rough stone column probably thirty feet above the road, on a grassy hillside. Arriving at the top, Kelsey and I leaned our bikes against the wall of a little *rifùgio*. Connie greeted us, and we all walked up a short eminence to the cross.

The column rises from a crude foundation of large, flat stones. Cemented to the base of that foundation, mountain grasses and wildflowers crowding in on it, was a modest, beautiful marble rectangle into which had been engraved:

IN MEMORY OF OUR FRIEND DAMON PHINNEY
3-4-1928   10-21-2001

We'd heard that Damon was memorialized somewhere at the summit, but had no idea that there was such a beautiful monument. Larry Theobald and Heather Reid—from the Breaking Away tour days—had followed through on their vow to "do something" for their friend. They knew a guy in Italy who created funeral monuments, and commissioned this one. They put it in the back of a van, with the help of a couple of clients, drove into France, and wrestled it up the hill to the base of the Croix. Thus did I find myself, on Father's Day, flooded with a torrent of emotions.

There was a mild sting of vestigial grief—I'll always feel that—but it was overwhelmed by a sublime sense of gratitude. I was thankful for the time we shared—especially the years since his Awakening. And I was grateful for his example. Indeed, my presence on that pass, in cycling kit, served as proof that I'd learned his greatest lesson: a chronic illness is not an excuse to stop living one's life, but rather, a call to start living it and embracing it more fully. My daily victories are a testament to him.

I felt his presence *so* strongly that, not surprisingly, I wept tears of joy and sorrow. Damon, the rocket scientist, did not hold to traditional Christian beliefs and much less to those of eternal life. Yet I couldn't escape the feeling that he was there—that, on some level, in some dimension, his son, and grandson (and granddaughter, and beloved daughter-in-law) had followed his wheel up the Croix de Fer that day.

The lead pack of riders had disappeared around a bend. By the time they burst back into view several switchbacks below, Taylor had caught the lead group and was working his way to the front.

Epilogue

AYLOR'S JOURNEY CONTINUES to enthrall. He won the prologue at the prestigious 2010 Tour de l'Avenir (Tour of the Future), then shook hands with Bernard Hinault, who pulled the leader's jersey over his head. Two days later he crashed badly, flaying a considerable amount of skin off the left side of himself but staying in the race. After leading the race, he finished second to last (like his old man on the Alpe d'Huez two decades earlier), earning respect for his perseverance, his *cou-RAHJ.*

Of course, when you're Taylor, the good moments far outnumber the bad. Earlier in the year, he won his second straight world title in the pursuit event in Denmark, and took a bronze in the newly added Omnium event. He won the criterium of a New Mexico stage race called the Tour of the Gila, in the process beating his boss, Lance Armstrong, in what would be their final race together. After squandering a victory by crashing near the end of the time trial at a Belgian race called the Triptyque des Monts et Châteaux—T led by 30 seconds when he went down—he was so ticked off that he went out and won the road stage that afternoon. A week after taking a ridiculous *four* stages, and the overall victory, in a national Dutch race called the Olympia's Tour, he won the U23 Paris-Roubaix — becoming the only rider to double in that event. The fitness gained from persevering in the Tour de l'Avenir in September was instrumental in giving him the power to beat veteran Levi Leipheimer — bronze medalist in the Beijing Olympic time trial — at the US Pro Championships. T won that thirty-three-kilometer race by 0.14 seconds, becoming the youngest US professional champion ever.

Taylor had such a stellar 2010, in fact, that by the end of August he had five teams from the Pro Tour — cycling's Major League — courting him with seriously lucrative offers, which eventually lured him out from under Lance's wing. It was time. The mentor was on the verge of retirement (again), and had retreated to work and family life. The future of his pro team, RadioShack, appeared tenuous. Armstrong's mentorship of Taylor was best in its nascence — those months after Beijing when T was struggling to find purpose, to find himself. Axel Merckx guided him through those early races, took it easy on him when he was sick or injured, and pushed him to historic victories. Taylor was, and remains, grateful for that support, which he used as a springboard.

So he signed with BMC. While cycling is a sport that doesn't advertise pro salaries, Taylor's agent, Andrew McQuaid, believes his multiyear deal with BMC could be the highest ever for a neo-pro. For me, it's a homecoming: the BMC program is run by my old boss, Jim Ochowicz. Och and Connie were both in Australia to watch T bring down the curtain on his 2010 season by taking the gold medal in the U23 world time trial championships.

The kid wins a lot, and I can't help noticing that when he does cross the line first, he holds his arms not so much up, in a V, but outstretched, like a lowercase t, as if to include the crowd in his celebration. It's less triumphal than my signature gesture, more inclusive, somehow — more generous, as if he's just bestowed a gift that he wants to share with the world. That, at least, is how this proud father sees it.

Acknowledgments

T HE GENESIS OF this book came several years ago, in Marin, with a spark from longtime friend Austin Murphy, who felt compelled to help tell my story. Thanks first and foremost to Austin for the spark, the fuel, the expertise, and the endurance to get it done.

Putting the stories to paper — that was the goal, and it was spurred by my desire to not lose them as I have lost much to the course of this disease. I wanted to share them not only with my children but with my tribe — my brethren — those of us who suffer from Parkinson's disease or live with any chronic debilitating illness — and with all of you — cycling fans, sports fans — whatever category you fall under.

There have been so very many people who've shaped, influenced, and helped me along the way; I'd like to acknowledge a few of the key players in my life.

I am grateful to my parents, Damon and Thea Phinney (aka Dad and Mom), for supporting my ambition, as counterintuitive as it must have seemed to them at the time, and to my brilliant, loving sister, Alice.

My childhood friends had a role in shaping me early on, including Betsy Chronic, Peter Thron, Clayton McMillan, Doug Addison, Frank Black, John LeCoq, Neil (Casey) King, Bill Elwood, Cathy (Tinka) Evans, Colleen Lang, John Metzger, Tom Holdridge, Bob Schmatz, and Ann Grunklee.

Thanks to school coaches Max McMillan, for teaching me one of my most valued life lessons, and classmate Carl Worthington, for all he's done and continues to do for youth sports.

To all the various team personnel that supported me — from the US national and Olympic teams to the Coors Light Cycling Team — and especially the groundbreaking 7-Eleven Cycling Team — a huge thank-you. Key staff included my visionary friend and former team manager Jim Ochowicz, team physician Max Testa, PR liaison Sean Petty, Coors team director Len Pettyjohn, mechanics George Noyes, Mike Hanley, Rich Gilstrap, Pat Rollins, Bob Gregorio, Eric Greene, Steve Mosher, soigneurs Shelley Verses, Trudi (Roberts) Rebsamen, Monica Van Haute, Julie Testa, John Hendershot, Nancy (Schierholt) Patterson, Patty Spiller, and Charlie Livermore — just a few of the many who made life significantly easier during my cycling career and beyond.

Thanks to the best teammates and friends I could ever have hoped for, including Ron Kiefel, Tom Schuler, Doug Shapiro, Alex Stieda, Eric Heiden, Andy Hampsten, Steve Bauer, Bob Roll, Chris Carmichael, Jeff Pierce, Sean Yates, Ron Hayman, Greg Demgen, Jeff Bradley, Jonathan Boyer, Andy Weaver, Roy Knickman, Dag Otto Lauritzen, Jens Veggerby, Danny Van Haute, and Scott McKinley — all with 7-Eleven. And to Ray Browning, Bjorn Laukli, Mike Engleman, Tom Chew, Tony Comfort, John Bowen, and many more — with whom I shared much and without whom I would not have won nearly as many races nor had nearly as much fun.

The Chew family and Bob Firth gave me a welcoming home and springboard when I needed it early in my career. Coach Eddie B., and enigmatic team directors Mike Neal and Noel Dejonckheere, proved learned, if sometimes maddening, teachers. Michael Aisner helped define my career and redefined American bike racing through his direction of the Coors Classic. I'm grateful to Ben Serotta for building me the finest bikes.

Bob Cook believed in me and influenced me deeply—and will never be forgotten. Other friends we have lost: Kristian Norman, Rick Beswick, Ed Burke, and Jim Owens—are deeply missed.

Charlie and Darcy Carpenter welcomed me into their family, and Darcy, in particular, set the bar high in terms of living gracefully with a chronic illness. Thanks to Chuck, Bob, and Jim Carpenter for embracing me as well.

We learned the true meaning of family and the importance of connectedness during our three years living in northern Italy, an experience that would not have been possible without the inspiration of the Zinn family, the support, guidance, and friendship of Steve and Krista Smith, and the always helpful Tim Maloney. Grazie moltissimo alla famiglia Parise per tutto. Abbraci e baci (hugs and kisses) to Daniela and Gianni, Francesco, Alberto and Angela, Fabrizio and Mara Salvini, and to Francesca Eger and the English International School in Rosà. We are very grateful to Monica and Rhiad at the Albergo Due Mori, and to the extended US Marosticense calcio community for embracing our children and welcoming us into their fold. Dai tosi!

Taylor's meteoric rise, and assault on Beijing, was made possible by a veritable team of experts and supporters. Thanks to Wayne Stetina, who prompted Jonathan Vaughters to give the unproven Taylor a chance in 2005. Thanks to Doug Ellis, and to Felt Bicycles, for their support. Coaches Neal Henderson, Roger Young, Allen Lim, Jim Miller, Ben Sharp, Simon Jones, and the entire New Zealand track team led by Craig Adair—all proved invaluable, as did the USA Cycling Foundation, and, in particular, Mick Hellman.

We are thankful to the entire Trek/Livestrong organization; especially Lance Armstrong, Bart Knaggs, and team director Axel

Merckx, who provided timely mentorship and motivation. And to Trek CEO John Burke for his commitment and vision; to Steve Hed for his expertise and devotion to aerodynamics; and to Ben Coates for his attention to detail, work ethic, and friendship.

We are excited by the prospect of Taylor's new association with the BMC Racing Team and owner Andy Rihs, as well as once again working directly with team co-owner Jim Ochowicz and his talented squad.

Without Andy Pruitt and the Boulder Center for Sports Medicine, we'd be nowhere. He has been a true friend to the entire Phinney family for more than three decades.

I'm grateful to Lance, Jeff Garvey, Joe Aragona, Livestrong, and the Lance Armstrong Foundation for inspiring millions of people, including my father, to fight the hard fight. Special thanks to Chris Brewer and Will Swetnam for helping create and sustain my dad's vision, Cyclists Combating Cancer (ridetolive.org).

The Davis Phinney Foundation has been a labor of love. Dr. John Tew was the iconic driving force in the creation of the DPF, which Kathy Krumme and David Ariosa, through their efforts and devotion, turned into a reality. Lorinn Rhodes took a leap of faith with us at the beginning, while Rick Tallman came in with early creative leadership. Kristie Henderson proved vital, and gave the foundation momentum and national presence through her hard work and marketing acumen. The vision and commitment to the tribe of current executive director Amy Howard have seen the DPF flourish. I owe them all, and everyone on the DPF staff, a debt of gratitude. Thanks for the unfailing friendship and guidance of Liz Snowden and Joe Tallman — and to the entire DPF board — in particular, our indefatigable chairman, Scott Coe; to the donors for supporting the work we do; and for the people living with PD, their caregivers, and clinicians around the world who embrace our motto: Every Victory Counts!

Thanks to Claude Pepin for introducing me to the possibilities of deep brain stimulation surgery, and to Medtronic, for pioneering the miraculous brain-pacemaker device. I feel incredibly fortunate to have met Dr. Jaimie Henderson and Dr. Helen Bronte-Stewart, with Stanford University Hospital — and I am forever thankful for their passion, expertise, and friendship. Thanks to my Denver-based neurologist, Dr. Olga Klepitskaya, my acupuncturist Dr. Ming Zhou, and chiropractor Dr. Steve Melis, who, along with Helen and her Stanford staff, keep me running smoothly.

My surgery, recovery, and subsequent well-being would not have been as stress-free and successful without the stalwart support of Monique Petrov, the continuing hospitality of Jim and Sheila Ochowicz in Palo Alto and Carl Weissensee and Candice Curtis in Tiburon, and the positive influence and generous spirit of Mara Rieden. Boulder friends who support us in all ways include Rick and Dayna Greenleaf, David and Wan Grabb, and Drew and Toni Geer.

Thanks and appreciation to longtime friend Frank Matson and Citizen Pictures, who documented the surgery, as well as put together various vignettes for the DPF. And to Graham Watson, John Kelly, Liz Kreutz, Peggy Dyer, John Pierce, and Robert Beck for so artfully photographing the journey. Thanks to our literary agent David Black for his belief, and our publishing editor Susan Canavan for her expertise.

To Taylor and Kelsey: This disease has not been easy on either of you, yet you've shown such an amazing amount of love, grace, and patience throughout the journey — all the while providing me with an infinite source of pride and daily joy.

And Connie. You have been the driving force in my life for thirty years, and so naturally you were the driving force behind seeing this project to completion. Thank you for your understanding, your humor, your compassion, and most of all, your enduring love.